THEN THEY WERE "ONE"

FUSION WITHOUT ABREACTION VIA THE "AS IF" TECHNIQUE IN 60 SECONDS OR LESS AN INNOVATIVE APPROACH TO THE DIAGNOSIS & TREATMENT OF DISSOCIATIVE IDENTITY DISORDER

BY EARL W. FLORA, PSY.D.

Copyright November 2014 Earl W. Flora, Psy.D.

This book remains the copyrighted property of the author, and may not be reproduced, copied and distributed for commercial or non-commercial purposes. Thank you for your support.

Cover photo and design by Earl W. Flora, Psy.D.

FOR INFORMATION CONTACT:

Earl W. Flora, Psy.D.
PO Box 564
Norge, VA 23127

Email: efquest@hotmail.com

Earl Flora

DISCLAIMER

The author and publisher repudiate any responsibility for unfavorable effects that results from, information, recommendations, undetected omissions or errors. This book is written for the exclusive use of mental health professionals and not for the general public! Discretion should be used especially by novice clinicians. Consultation and supervision are highly recommended with professionals who are well schooled in the diagnosis and treatment of Dissociative Identity Disorder (DID). It is not the purpose of this book to provide all the information that is otherwise available on the subject of DID, but instead to complement, amplify, and supplement other texts. All professionals using this book are encouraged to research all available sources of authority as well.

Earl Flora

DEDICATION

I dedicate this book to my loving wife, Nancy Mary Jane Flora, with my deepest appreciation. Without her inspiration and support this book would never have been written.

Earl Flora

ACKNOWLEDGMENT

I want to acknowledge Vernon Grounds, B.A., B.D. and Ph.D., who taught the class on pastoral counseling at the Conservative Baptist Theological Seminary in Denver, Colorado, where he was the president, later to be named chancellor, for his words of encouragement. He became my role model and inspiration, without ever knowing it. This work would never have happened without his positive influence in my choice of careers.

I also, most heartily, want to thank those brave souls, without whom this book would never have been possible, who placed their trust in me to find meaning and purpose in their lives by resolving their separateness and allowing them to finally say, "For the first time in my life I know who I am!" It is only through their courage, determination and cooperation that the "As If" procedure was achieved and validated over the past 27 years. I hasten to say, "This continues to be a work in progress." Finally, I want to thank an anonymous donor for her generous financial support. I hasten to say, "This continues to be a work in progress."

Earl Flora

PREFACE

The ultimate question the client asks is, "Can you help me?" In keeping with the spirit of the Hippocratic Oath, the next query follows, "Can you help me without doing harm?" And the third inquiry is from the therapist him/herself, "Is there a better way?" The impulse that drives these interrogatories becomes professional mandates, of course, and each is relevant to this new text. It is well that you have taken Dr. Earl Flora's description of his technique in hand.

For 27 years, Dr. Flora has ably and effectively served those suffering from Dissociative Identity Disorder/Multiple Personality Disorder (DID/MPD), winning him the appreciation and esteem of his patients, colleagues, clergy and social servants. "Then They Were One," in practice, has proven to be decisively effective but, most importantly, a warmly appreciated approach by his clients.

This beautiful, redemptive, healing therapy certainly deserves a hearing among mental health professionals. The aim is simple: to ease the pain of personality fusion and advance the effectiveness of the attempt, a purpose no one could be against. Those not moved will call it radical or worse. Those who take the method to heart will catch a whiff of a humane revolution in the air. And, refreshed by this innovation, still others will embrace it as a renaissance in the treatment of DID/MPD.

Dr. Flora is quick to affirm there is nothing original in the ground from which his technique arises only, perhaps, the application of it. He also is attempting to communicate with colleagues who have worked along similar lines and with similar effectiveness because he, like others, wants to improve technique for the sake of those he serves.

Earl Flora

I applaud what he describes here. It is positive, not negative; forward, not backward looking; helpful and not punishing. It reflects an absolute concern for the person and affirms they have attempted to deal with things the best they could. It insists on a creative integration rather than burning down parts of the personality that, after admitting their limits, even dysfunction, actually offer tremendous strengths. The technique would be aptly likened to adoption and integration rather than abortion.

He brings his faith perspective to the table, but it is done fairly. It would be incomplete without it and certainly would not address the faith perspective of so many of his clients without it. On the other hand, I think he has offered a meaningful forum for discussing this with colleagues from a secular perspective.

The reader will enjoy how the author's transparent narrative and explanation introduce us at once to an erudite scholar, pragmatist, and professional who's impatient with stodgy, unreflective peers in the profession, and is a fierce advocate for those who suffer. And, therefore, as you would expect, it follows that the imagery offered herein is quite lively, both the insightful illustrations to help the reader understand, as well as the imagery employed in therapy for the clients' sake. It's easily understood and its helpfulness fully acceptable.

In short, what follows is exciting, some parts poignant and others great fun, but a great read and full of hope.

James B. Johnson II, Ed.D. M.Div.
August 29, 2014

CONTENTS

DISCLAIMER 3
DEDICATION 5
ACKNOWLEDGMENT 7
PREFACE 9
CONTENTS 11
CHAPTER ONE - PERSONAL BACKGROUND 16
CHAPTER TWO - INTRODUCTION 18
CHAPTER THREE - HISTORICAL BACKGROUND 22
    The Problem 22
    The Beginnings 22
    The Rise of Disintegrated Personality, aka DID 25
CHAPTER FOUR – DEFINITIONS 27
    Dissociative 27
    Dissociative 27
    DID Characteristics 29
    Internal Co-therapist 31
    The Subconscious Mind 31
    Multiple: 32
    Alter/personality 32
    Fusion 32
    Integration 32
    Co-conscious 32
    Protector/Guardian 32
    Synergism 32
    Original Personality 33
    Presenting Personality 33

Core Personality 33
Fusion 33
Trial Fusion 33
"As If" 33
Abreaction 33
Interjects 34
Reverse Installation 34
Oneness vs. Divided Mind 34
Soul/Souls 35
Coalescence 38
True Identity 38

CHAPTER FIVE - THE CHALLENGE 39

CHAPTER SIX - THE PROCESS 41
Introduction: 41
The "As If" ceremony from a Christian perspective 44
A Secular variation of the "As If" Fusion Ceremony 46
Variations leading up to the "As If" Ceremony: 47

CHAPTER SEVEN - TRANSITIONAL CASE EXAMPLES 49
Case #1: 49
Case # 2: 51
Case #3: 53
Case # 4: 55

CHAPTER EIGHT – DISCUSSION - RESISTANCE TO CHANGE
.... 63

CHAPTER NINE - SPECIAL TECHNIQUES 65
Interjects 65
Cult induced interjects 65
Therapist-induced interject 67
Exorcism: Demon possession 68

Example of a church-sponsored exorcism with a DID 70
My first encounter with a "demon" or so he said 71
Homicidal alters, not interjects 72
Closely related trauma 74
ALTERS REFUSING TO JOIN THE CORE 74
Example One: 75
Example Two: 76
Observation: Dissociation is the result of negative affect. 77
A word of encouragement, "I'm tired of being alone, I'm ready."
.... 78

CHAPTER TEN - ALTERS CREATING PROBLEMS 79
Case #1 79
Case #2 80
Case #3 82
Case #4 83
Case #5 86
Case #6 88
Case #7 90

CHAPTER ELEVEN - SITUATIONS TO AVOID 93
Case #1 93
Case #2 95

CHAPTER TWELVE - VALIDATION 97
PROBLEMS: 97
ANSWERS: 97
To the first criticism: Iatrogenesis 97
To the second criticism: False memories 98
To the third criticism: Figment of imagination 98

CHAPTER THIRTEEN - STRANGE SITUATIONS 101
First example 101

Second example 101
Third example 102
Fourth example 103
Fifth example 106
Sixth example 108
Seventh example 109
Eighth example 110
Ninth example 111
Tenth example 112
Eleventh example 114
Twelfth example 117
Thirteenth example 121
Fourteenth example 121
Fifteenth example 122
Sixteenth example 125
CHAPTER FOURTEEN - TESTIMONIALS 127
A Husband's Experience 127
A Successfully Integrated Female 129
The First and Longest Successful Intergration 130
A Married Nurse and Mother 131
A Middle-aged Married Mother Approaching the End of the Intergration Process on Becoming Whole 135
CHAPTER FIFTEEN - INTERVIEW, DIAGNOSIS AND TREATMENT 141
Interview/Diagnosis 141
Treatment (not necessarily in this order): 142
CHAPTER SIXTEEN - POSTLUDE 155
APPENDIX 157
INDIVIDUAL DISSOCIATION IDENTITY CHECK LIST ... 157

EXTERNAL DISSOCIATION IDENTITY CHECK LIST
OBSERVED BY OTHERS 158
REFERENCES 161
INDEX 166

Earl Flora

CHAPTER ONE - PERSONAL BACKGROUND

As of this writing, there are 101 books currently listed on Barnes & Noble's website on the subject of Dissociative Identity Disorder/Multiple Personality Disorder (DID/MPD) and hundreds of articles on the subject. As such, I do not intend to reproduce material already published. Rather, I will present what has worked for those entrusted to my care. In addition, I will share insights gained along the way because things are not always what they seem to be.

My professional experience includes being a senior psychologist for one year at Southwestern Virginia Mental Health Institute in Marion, Virginia. I was the psychologist supervisor in the Geriatric Treatment Center at Eastern State Hospital in Williamsburg, Virginia, for five years. During that time, for two semesters I was adjunct faculty at The College of William & Mary where I taught the section on multiple personality disorder. In 1990, I founded the Poplar Creek Psychological and Counseling Centre in Norge, Virginia, where I have been in private practice ever since. My clinical experience includes treating a wide range of clients from young to geriatric. During the past 20 years or so, at various times, I have provided onsite geriatric psychological services for 23 different nursing and rehabilitation facilities. For almost 30 years, I have been involved in the diagnosis and treatment of MPD/DID. Conservatively, I have diagnosed and treated well over 100 suffers. To be honest, I'm sorry to admit I was not keeping score, so I have lost count!

I have been laughed at, scorned and criticized by other clinicians, prosecutors, opposing counsel and physicians. I sat across from a satanic cult alter pointing a loaded nine-shot 22- caliber revolver at me with instructions to kill me by the local satanic cult. By the grace of God, I was able to remain calm and switched, from him, to the female core personality by softly calling her name. She was shocked to find she was pointing a loaded gun at me. I explained the situation and asked if she would be interested in selling her gun to me. She agreed and I purchased it from her.

I testified in six DID forensic court cases including shoplifting, child custody, child sexual abuse and homicide. As it related to DID, I have read extensively, attended workshops, conferences, presented in-services and defended my doctoral dissertation, "Tracing the Historical Development of the Diagnosis and Treatment of Multiple Personality Disorder in 19th and 20th Century North America."

My educational background includes a bachelor's degree in Bible from the Philadelphia College of Bible (now Cairn University), a bachelor's in psychology from Florida International University, a master's degree and a doctor of psychology degree with distinction from the Miami Institute of Psychology of the Caribbean Center for Advanced Studies (now Carlos Albizu University).

Because of such wide exposure, I am certain I have incorporated various techniques learned from other therapists. Where I am aware of the source, I will gratefully acknowledge it. I attempt to explain how I processed the information, which led to what I am about to share with you.

I do not claim to have any original theories — just, maybe, original conclusions. I offer readers an account of my therapeutic techniques, with the expectation, as they are implemented will ease, if not eliminate the re-traumatizing pain caused by abreaction for those brave souls who place themselves in our care. I also want to be sure to mention that many therapists/counselors experience increased countertransference when they implement abreaction to effect fusion. I have never experienced any countertransference using the "As If" fusion technique. I maintain that this technique is a win-win situation for both client and therapist!

CHAPTER TWO - INTRODUCTION

You ask why another book on Dissociative Identity Disorder (DID)? The answer can be found on any search engine DID forum. There are many dedicated, hardworking mental health professionals utilizing various systems to diagnose and treat this phenomenon. As far as I can tell, none of the above is exactly like the "As If" system. The system I will be presenting has evolved over 27 years and has stood the test of time. The tried-and-true system avoids abreaction caused by forcing the "limited life-experienced alters" to relive the trauma over and over until they have been desensitized. This is, in effect, the "in-vivo desensitization" I was taught in graduate school. It was too exhausting for both client and therapist to undertake alone, if ever. The result is the same, "integration;" however, the "negative affect" is not processed. Rather it is removed—in most cases painlessly and in a few, almost painlessly. As with abreaction, once the negative affect is removed the result is spontaneous fusion. I, as have others, observed the "negative affect" to be the "amnestic barrier." So, once the negative affect is removed, one by one the amnestic barriers disappear, until there are none.

As therapy progresses, barriers dissolve, necessitating the subconscious mind to begin adapting alternative coping techniques. Fusion in itself is mechanical and final. This is not to suggest that clients, who have just acquired very negative, earlier life experiences, are happy to learn they were abused earlier in their lives, perhaps by significant family members. However, being assimilated into the "greater life experience" does not appear to be re-traumatizing, even though there can be a tolerable level of sadness and mixed feelings to be processed. The "As If" technique does not prevent the client from being able to experience a normal range of affect. Adjusting to newly acquired life experiences and adapting new coping techniques is the ongoing therapy, even after final integration, for an extended period of time. After all, the only constant in everyone's life is change.

In CHAPTER SIX, I will explain how the process was developed, as well as the theory behind it in greater detail.

In CHAPTER SEVEN, I will present four case studies involved in the transition from the old process to the new process. In the new process, fusion of individual and groups of alters was accomplished without the widely used technique referred to as "abreaction." By combining a variation of the hypnotic "As If" "time progression to a positive outcome" technique, Carich (1991) and Vaihinger (1968), along with the self-fulfilling prophesy metaphor "time heals all wounds," all acquired life experiences (positive and negative) held by the alter begin to fall into chronological order at the moment of fusion with the core personality. Depending on individual differences, I have observed coalescence can range from immediately to more than a few weeks. One client reported assimilating acquired experiences at night in her dreams.

In the TESTIMONIAL CHAPTER FOURTEEN, I include personal testaments from several successful integrations who were the result of the new "As If" system. In addition, a husband, who was very supportive during a rather protracted process, provides glimpses as to what he experienced and how his life has benefited from his wife's successful integration. In all these cases, you will read their personal testimonies as to how their lives have changed for the better. (Note: Names are changed to protect their privacy.)

I will share various techniques which have proven helpful in dealing with resistance and aggressive/controlling alters/interjects.

For the sake of continuity and space, I have taken the liberty of editing sparingly, without changing the content or context, when citing session contents. While every effort has been made to disguise individuals, it may be possible to identify someone.

All session references, of any length, are printed with permission. However, all names have been changed, as well as the names of the alter states of consciousness (aka, personalities), to ensure privacy. All quotes will be in italics and quotation marks.

Earl Flora

(Note: I will explain why I referred to DID as a phenomenon, later in the Definitions Section.)

Then They Were One

CHAPTER THREE - HISTORICAL BACKGROUND

The Problem

I am including a brief history of DID for those who are new to the concept and any who might need evidence as to its authenticity. I must admit in the beginning I thought I was crazy for believing what I was seeing. I was waiting for somebody to throw a net over my head and haul me away to a locked ward in a mental health facility. Having thus said, a healthy skepticism is the sign of an intelligent mind. All I ask from skeptics is that they keep an open mind because, in the end, it's always the truth that prevails.

DID, aka, MPD has had a stormy and controversial history. From its beginning to the present-day, there have been problems associated with the conceptualization, diagnosis and treatment of DID as separate and distinct from all other psychological disorders.

In an attempt to offer some rationale to this problem, literature from the 19th and 20th century is reviewed to provide historical continuity. DID's development, as it relates to its etiology, diagnosis and treatment, is traced in an effort to explain its birth, growth in the 1800s, decline and nearly demise in the early 1900s, and obvious period of great activity during the latter half of the 20th century with increasing interest up to the present.

The Beginnings

As stated above, from the very beginning DID has been a lesson in contrasts and controversy, as illustrated by the ebb and flow of interest over the past two-plus centuries. The historical account of DID is linked with hysteria, artificial somnambulism (e.g., mesmerism/hypnosis) and for centuries the decline in the phenomenon, which is known as possession in many parts of the world.

Hysteria extends all the way back to the ancient Egyptians and Greeks. Hippocrates recorded a case of hysteria and connected its etiology to a wandering uterus (Bliss, 1980). Hysterical psychosis-type traits (e.g., social isolation, self-mutilation, aggressive behavior, screaming and uncontrolled crying) are seen in the actions of the man possessed by demons as recorded in the Bible (Mark 5:1-20). The Diagnostic and Statistical Manual of Mental Disorders, IV-TR (DSM-IV-TR), incorporates the same behaviors under the diagnostic criteria for a Hysterical Neurosis, Dissociative Type with psychotic features (Note: since dropped in the DSM-5).

By the early 1780s, "induced somnambulism" was popularized as the result of Franz Anton Mesmer demonstrating the effects of "animal magnetism." In 1843, James Braid would change the name to hypnotism, a derivation of the Greek "hypnotikos" meaning sleep-inducing narcotic. (Random House Dictionary of the English Language, Unabridged, 1966.) Between 1810 and 1830, the first attempts to bring the phenomenon of hypnosis into the scientific camp, such as it was, were made when Alexandre Bertrand published his two books, "Traité du Somnambulism" ("Sleepwalking Facts") in 1823 and "Du Magnétisme Animal en France" ("Of Animal Magnetism in France") in 1826. From about 1840 to 1850 mesmerism was the "in thing." Mesmer's followers were holding meetings and conventions, giving and receiving awards and prizes. (Ellenberger, 1970)

Unfortunately, popularity also has its price, and so it was that as Mesmer's followers increased in quantity, they decreased in quality. Mesmer's disciples engaged in wild speculation, occultism and even out-and-out quackery (Ellenberger, 1970). During "the period from 1860 to 1880, magnetism and hypnotism had fallen into such disrepute that a physician working with these methods would irretrievably have compromised his scientific career and lost his medical practice." (Ellenberger, 1970, p. 85)

By the end of 1880 hypnosis was enjoying a resurgence of popularity, reaching a new milestone with Jean-Martin Charcot's reading of his famous paper on the three successive stages of hypnosis: "lethargy, catalepsy and somnambulism" (Note: Since proven wrong.) to the Académie des Sciences in 1882.

This was significant since the Académie had rejected hypnotism three times in the past (Charcot cited in Ellenberger, 1970). It was into this setting that a detailed description and explanation for the condition was first attempted.

The concept of "possession" played an important role in the development of DID. Its roots are recorded in the Bible when Jesus cast out demons at Gerasa (Mark 5: 1-20) and the disciples cast out many demons (as recorded in Mark 6:13) during the time of Jesus.

There is a strong possibility that DID coexisted with possession for thousands of years, only to go undetected. By definition, "possession" could be considered a type of DID. A possessed person would suddenly lose his/her sense of identity and start acting like another person.

In possession, the belief in "embodiment" is paramount, so that possessed people's physical appearance would change to resemble that of the one's who supposedly possess them. They often spoke in different voices. It was common for them to exhibit the ability to perform amazing feats of strength. States of possession usually occurred spontaneously, fluctuating in frequency, duration and intensity.

Somnambulistic possession is a state of sudden unconsciousness, the emergence of a foreign spirit speaking in the first person singular "I" and amnestic for the preceding events upon regaining consciousness (Ellenberger, 1970). Spontaneous possession is outside the individual's control. Usually, "…it is a specific mental condition from which the patient seeks relief with the help of the exorcist" (Ellenberger, 1970, p. 14).
Then there is the voluntary possession when the individual seeks to be possessed for a secondary gain (e.g., shamans, witch doctors, mediums and speaking in tongues).

It is easy to see the parallels between spirit possession and DID (e.g., loss of control of one's body, the possibility of co-consciousness in some cases and not in others, amnesia, and sensing the presence of someone or something else inside you). They both possess the quality of being either observable or concealed.

The Rise of Disintegrated Personality, aka DID

During the 19th century, it was only after the decline of the phenomenon known as "possession" that case histories involving "dissociated personalities" — or to use Morton Prince's (1906/1969) "*disintegrated* personality" (p. 8) — started turning up in mesmerist literature and later in medical reports (Ellenberger, 1970). Historically DID has been considered rare (DSM-III, 1980 and Thigpen and Cleckley, 1984). Taylor and Martin (1944) indicated that only 93 cases of DID were reported between 1817 and 1972. In 1955 psychiatrist Dr. Cornelia Wilbur was under the impression, after reviewing the literature, that there were only two cases reported. Between 1970 and 1981, more than 80 cases were cited (Graves, 1980, and Boor, 1982). By 1987, over 1,800 cases had been seen by some 217 clinical psychologists, psychiatrists and other mental health professionals (Rose, Norton and Wozney, 1987).

It's not difficult to discover the culprit for the, almost, disappearance of DID patients in the early 1900s. After psychiatrist Kurt Schneider published his first-rank systems for schizophrenia in 1938 (Oxford University Press, Oxford Index), DID virtually disappeared from the clinical population, under the misdiagnosis of schizophrenia. It's sad to say, even though it's understandable, that today many DID clients/patients still are misdiagnosed as schizophrenic by the mental health community due to lack of training. These first-rank symptoms for the diagnosis of schizophrenia better diagnose DID and are included in several DID system checklists, including mine.

By the end of the 20th century, approximately 40,000 DID cases had been diagnosed (Maldonado, JR; Spiegel D (2008), Lynn, SJ; Berg J; Lilienfeld SO; Merckelbach H; Giesbrecht T; Accardi M; Cleere C 2012).

Finally, with the publication of the American Psychiatric Association's Diagnostic and Statistical Manual of Mental Disorders 5 (DSM-5), in June 2013, the mental health community has added a subheading, "Prevalence. The 12-month prevalence of dissociative identity disorder among adults in a small U.S. community study was 1.5 percent. The prevalence across genders in the study was 1.6 percent for males and 1.4 percent for females."(DSM-5, p. 294)

Now if we compare these statistics with those for schizophrenia found on page 102 in the DSM-5, "The life time prevalence of schizophrenia appears to be approximately 0.3 percent - 7 percent." Depending on which statistics you use, DID can be as high as two times more prevalent as schizophrenia. Yet it has less literature and less acceptance than schizophrenia, which is chronic and can, at best, be somewhat controlled with strong psychotropic medications. Whereas, barring comorbidity, DID requires no medication to fully resolve the dissociative problem. In the "As If" system, I will describe how fusion and integration are accomplished using talking therapy alone.

Now back to the statistics: By dividing 1.5 percent into the various population figures you get the following DID populations on 02/06/2014:

World Population: 7,141,000,000/1.5 = 107,115,000 DID individuals

U.S. Population: 316,148,990/1.5 = 4,742,234 DID individuals

James City County, VA (my county), population: 68,967/1.5 = 1,034 DID individuals

Williamsburg, Va., population: 15,167/1.5 = 227 DID individuals
I have to state it in bold caps, **"THIS IS HARDLY A SMALL SUFFERING POPULATION!"**

I challenge you to do the math for your location.

CHAPTER FOUR – DEFINITIONS

I understand it's normal to put definitions in the back of the book in the section titled Glossary. If this is abnormal then so be it. Before we go any further, I think it's important to define the terms I'll be using throughout the text. I realize there are various descriptions used by others for the one's I'll be presenting. This isn't to suggest that I alone possess the absolute authority to define terms. What is important is the reader use the same definitions I use when coming across various terms in the text. That is not to say you have to agree with my conclusions, only that you understand what I have in mind. Various words and phrases are italicized to emphasize their importance in understanding how I treat DID.

Dissociative Identity Disorder (DSM 5): To save space, if you are interested, check out the American Psychiatric Association's 2013 Diagnostic and Statistical Manual of Mental Disorders 5 (DSM 5) p. 292 for its definition of DID.

Dissociative Identity Disorder (my definition): As for DID's etiology, I believe DID is the direct result of the overdevelopment of one of the primary defense mechanisms common to humans and other life forms, characterized as "Dissociation." It is even found in the animal kingdom, most notably, in the marsupial known as the opossum, colloquially called simply "possum," that is known for "playing possum." It appears to be innate, found in One's deoxyribonucleic acid (DNA). In the case of the opossum, the reaction seems to be involuntary and triggered by extreme fear.

We are born with the ability to dissociate on a continuum, but for some unknown reason, some people are born with an overactive ability to dissociate. I have treated more than one intergenerational family members with DID, (e.g., grandmother/mother/daughter and mother/son combinations). Through this phenomenon, individuals unconsciously use their imagination to detach themselves from unpleasant, seemingly life-threatening occurrences by compartmentalizing (e.g., causing an amnestic barrier to be erected) the traumatizing event in the subconscious mind.

Earl Flora

Not only major traumatic events can cause the event to be compartmentalized. Sometimes a relatively minor event in childhood — such as being startled by a loud noise, being left crying in the crib too long, having a toy taken away, being belittled by their playmates, being criticized by their parents, being separated from the primary caregiver for an extended period or parental divorce may be all it takes to drop the amnestic barrier in their young minds. These are only a few of the examples of seemingly insignificant events that have been dissociated over and over again.

In later years it can be the loss of a child, job, marriage, beloved friend or parent, a sudden change in one's health or a natural disaster to mention only a few of the situations I have witnessed that have caused amnestic barriers to be initiated at various stages of human development. The list is endless.

I have observed, over the past 27 years, all of us are born with the capacity to dissociate, but some of us do it too well. It begins as one of the primary defense mechanisms but soon can become the principal defense mechanism. Very interestingly, I have observed these individuals to be at the higher end of the intellectual scale.

One client described DID as "a child's game gone awry." I believe the subconscious mind interprets various life events, as they are too stressful for the conscious mind to handle. The subconscious mind believes the system could not survive with that much stress in the conscious mind.

To prevent the body from fainting or being paralyzed in a state of shock, an amnestic barrier is lowered in an instant, blocking prior life history from the "non-conscious mind." Since there is no past history available to the "now new-conscious mind," all it can do is observe the environment from that moment on to try and make sense out of the moment. The "now new-conscious mind" only lacks personal history. The "now new-conscious mind" is able to use the body to fulfill its physical needs. It has a vocabulary but no sense of personal identity to guide its use. Without history there is no wisdom, so decisions and actions take place almost helter-skelter, unless the inner voices guide and direct their actions.

Switching: Years ago, at a conference on dissociation, I remember the audience being admonished by Richard Kluft, M.D. not to focus on understanding the mechanism, but rather to focus on resolving the problem. That is still sage advice. However, over the years, communicating with the part of the mind that takes credit for switching from one level of consciousness to another I've asked, *"Just how do you do this?"*

In every case, with slight variations, the answer was the same, *"I don't know. I just do it and it happens."*

Another client said, *"All I do is say, 'She needs help. Do it now' and it happens. I think it's her brain that does it. I don't see anybody. It just happens."*

It has to be a conscious thought on the one hand, but then on the other hand, it appears to come from the true "subconscious mind." It sounds like they are using self-hypnosis techniques by internally configuring cognitive change. I am sure I am over-simplifying the process, but how else can we understand it from a behavior prospectus? It is not within the scope of this book to get bogged down with neurological explanations.

DID Characteristics: I have included a modified "Individual Dissociative Identity Check List" in the APPENDIX. I have compiled 30 different traits commonly seen in individuals experiencing DID. Most of these are found in various publications, but anyone working with DID would soon be able, without prior knowledge, to end up with more or less the same observations.

Also found in the APPENDIX is the "External Dissociative Identity Check List Observed by Others." This is very helpful to establish the validity of the diagnosis with a spouse or other family members. The usual response, once it is completed, is *"Oh, now she/he makes sense!"* In many cases these clients have been in the system for many years with no positive results. The look of relief on the faces of the relatives is priceless. For the first time their loved ONE is making sense.

Once I explain treatment is only "talking therapy" with a favorable prognosis they are very supportive and willingly participate in couple's and/or family sessions as necessary. (Note: See CHAPTER FOURTEEN, TESTIMONIALS: A HUSBAND'S EXPERIENCE.)

Also helpful in diagnosing DID in children is Dr. Frank W. Putnam's excellent "Child Dissociative Checklist" included in the APPENDIX.

Included in the characteristic check lists is a selection of Kurt Schneider's first-rank schizophrenic psychotic symptoms, mainly dealing with internal brain functions, as opposed to those referring to external stimulations. However, I do not consider these symptoms to be psychotic in the case of DID clients. The four systems are:

- Believing their behaviors are being controlled by forces beyond their control,
- Believing their thoughts are being controlled by forces beyond their control,
- Hearing internal voices that comment on their thoughts and/or actions, and
- Hearing internal conversation between two or more voices.

It is easy to differentiate between schizophrenic voices and DID voices. Schizophrenic voices do not respond to me, whereas DID voices respond to my direct question, *"Will an inner voice answer a question?"* Regardless whether the answer is *"Yes"* or *"No"* the fact that an answer is heard, spoken inside their head at all, pretty much nails the diagnosis. However, I never make the diagnosis until an "alter state of consciousness" comes out, identifies her/himself and speaks to me.

Internal Co-therapist (ICT/CT): Establishing a CT is absolutely essential in effecting a positive outcome. As soon as the diagnosis is confirmed, I ask, *"Is there anyone inside that would be willing to be my internal co-therapist and help me from the inside world, by answering various questions?"*

Almost without fail I get a quick affirmative reply. It is usually an adolescent alter who volunteers. Adolescent is the age children usually seek approval. I then explain that I will never lie to them or hurt them. All I ask is that she/he always answers truthfully even if she/he does not know the answer.

I establish three ways for my CT to respond: (1) verbally, internally to the alter in the conscious mind, (2) verbally to me, and (3) to use "ideomotor response" (Cheek, 1962) techniques where raising the thumb means yes, raising the index finger means no and wiggling the index finger means she does not know the answer.

The Subconscious Mind: It is not within the purpose of this book to solve the problem of defining and fully understanding the subconscious and/or unconscious mind. I do not want this to be a point of contention and distract from the main purpose of this endeavor "to relieve pain and suffering."

I perceive the subconscious mind to be part of the brain that is the reservoir of life's memories, learned behaviors and the seat of ones' intellect. In this capacity, it regulates all "higher" human functions. But it never overrides the conscious mind or takes over executive control.

Using established hypnotic techniques, I am able to verbally communicate directly with the subconscious mind. The subconscious mind is then able to respond directly to me by using a system of physical signals known as "ideomotor responses" (Cheek, 1962) in this case, finger movements to indicate "yes" with the thumb, "no" with the index finger and by wiggling the index finger "I don't know."

Earl Flora

On occasion I will ask the subconscious mind to tell my CT something, (e.g. "How much life experience does the core now contain?" or any question CT is not unable to answer. Once CT has the information, she passes it to the alter in the conscious mind, who verbally shares the information with me.

Multiple: At times, I will refer to my clients suffering from DID as "multiples." Whenever I refer to a client as a "multiple" I am writing about the "whole person."

Alter/personality: When I use the term "alter" or "personality," I am referring to a "compartmentalized part" of the whole person. It is my clinical experience, depending on the age of the client/patient, that the majority of the personalities are children.

Fusion: When I speak of "fusion" I mean the coming together of two or more alters by removing the amnestic barrier.

Integration: The coalescence (coming together) of life events which takes place after "fusion."

Co-conscious: It is self-explanatory but I like to visualize it like a double exposure or a simultaneous overlay of life experiences. In this state there is intermingling of life events, including the affect (e.g., If the alter had a headache the core will have a headache. If the alter has a fever the core will have a fever. Whatever the feeling — good, bad or indifferent — it will be projected onto the core).

Protector/Guardian: In almost every case, there are children alters that developed early in life. It appears they learned how to protect and/or control the other personalities by modeling their parents' and/or their abusers' behavior.

Synergism: I use the concept "the whole is greater than the sum of the parts" or "the combined action of two or more parts is greater than the sum of each acting separately" to help my client understand the ultimate advantage of becoming ONE mind.

Original Personality: This is the person prior to the first split usually in infancy. This is the alter the whole life experience is protecting.

Presenting Personality: This is the personality that first came into therapy.

Core Personality: This is the personality into which all other personalities join. She/he may be the personality that first came into therapy but not always. I negotiate with the entire system and let the system decide who the core personality will be. But in every case it is the personality into which the others join.

Fusion Ceremony: This is the ceremony administered once one or more alters agree to join the core, in which the amnestic barrier is dissolved and they become one. See the complete "As If" fusion ceremony in CHAPTER SIX

Trial Fusion: This is usually the first "As If" fusion ceremony. It's like a "test drive" to see if you like it. At this point in the therapy, One alter doesn't know what it's like to join another alter, so I offer them a way to join but not to stay joined if they don't like it. *This way they are in control.* I give each one the use of either the right or left hand, mainly the use of the thumb which signifies yes and/or the index finger denoting no. There must be two thumbs up to stay together. If either one extends the index finger, they will immediately come apart.

"As If": This is the lynchpin of the 'As If' fusion ceremony in which pseudo time distortion, age progression, posthypnotic suggestion culminate in a "self-fulfilling prophesy." (Note: No formal induction is initiated.)

Abreaction: In Freudian psychoanalysis, this is an episode of emotional release or catharsis associated with the conscious recollection of repressed unpleasant experiences. Catharsis is the process of rapidly releasing negative emotions, fully experiencing the pain and fear surrounding the incident.

Interjects: These are "pseudo alters" that take on the characteristics of actual earlier life experiences. They are modeled after living or dead individuals, animals or spirits/demons. They can be created by an internal dissociative process and/or outside forces like the satanic cult, other cults or unintentional suggestions made during therapy to these highly suggestible people. Since I believe these people are in a virtual state of self-hypnosis, I need to be very careful that I do not create interjects.

In my practice, I have come across the following interjects:

- Those placed in the mind by relevant people who may have a specific role outside of what would be the normal coping mechanism (e.g., be part of a satanic cult to participate in their rituals).
- Those placed in the mind that are actual copies of living or dead relatives/individuals by part of the mind I refer to as the "subconscious."
- Those placed in the mind by the therapist, either inadvertently or on purpose.

Reverse Installation: This is the technique I devised to erase interjects. It is simply reversing the process used to put them in the mind in the first place. I don't need to know what was said. I simply state with authority that "On the count of three — one, two, three — whatever process used to install you (Note: If I know the name, I use it. If there is no name, I use the operational description.) will, in reverse, begin slowly at first picking up speed continue to erase you until you are completely erased from the memory."

To check if the reverse installation was successful, I ask my inner co-therapist to "look all around and let me know if he/she is gone."

Oneness vs. Divided Mind: Alters see themselves as individuals, not sharing ONE body. They see the other alters as individuals, if they see them at all. They think everybody in the world is like them. The concept of "Oneness" is as foreign to them as the concept of a "Divided Mind" is to those of us who are of one mind.

As therapy progresses, they have a great deal of difficulty believing, understanding and accepting the concept of "Oneness," of not needing to dissociate or to go inside as they call it. I expect resistance to the concept by various alters. The resistance comes in many forms such as alters making them miss appointments, taking control of the car while driving to the sessions and taking them way out of the way, causing them to be late or miss the appointment altogether. They also can threaten bodily harm by cutting or burning the body with cigarettes if they continue to come to therapy. (Note: The tragedy is they do not realize they are hurting their own body.) Yes, and they can even threaten the therapist.

Soul/Souls: "Does each personality/alter have its own soul?"

To the best of my memory, this subject has never come up with any of my clients. It has never been a topic of discussion even between any of my theological friends. However, it has come up in DID literature. As such, drawing upon my formal Christian theological education I will give my considered opinion.

Answer: If we can agree we define a living human being as possessing one body with one set of extremities, one head, two arms and hands, two legs with feet and toes, one heart and one brain, that is not possessed by any demons, then taking the body as a collection of millions of cells, countless neurons, atoms, neutrons, protons, etc. and whatever years of existence recorded in the brain, then the only logical and theological conclusion would be one soul per body. (Note: Just in case anyone thinks I haven't considered it, things get a lot more confusing in the case of the two-headed person, but I think I'll leave that one up to the Divine to work out.)

Why the question at all?

Well if my concept is correct, there is one body, one soul and one brain/mind that records all life events. In the "mono (non-multiples) person," these life events are retrieved as what we call "our" memories. However, they are not always in chronicle order.

DIDs (MPDs) are capable of "compartmentalizing/dissociating" various short and/or extended life experiences as a function of their autonomic nervous system, (e.g., fight or flight). Dissociation, as their primary defense system, spontaneously separates off, into the subconscious mind, any event accompanied by what they determine to be excessive negative affect and, therefore, a mortal threat to their very existence. Over a period of time these compartmentalization's take on an existence/life of their own (Note: They are the accumulation of acquired "time-limited life events experienced" by the various alters) that can appear in the conscious mind, with or without names, taking complete control of the body.

If they were separate human beings/people, then by definition, they would possess their own souls. However, they are earlier life experiences that have become compartmentalized. They view themselves as autonomous, individual, separate beings possessing their own bodies and souls. (Note: That's where the real danger and dysfunction lies. They may encourage other alters to kill themselves not realizing they are also going to die!)

Question?

I am constantly asked to explain:

- What are these personas?
- Where did they come from?
- Why are they here?

I will start with trying to answer the second question first: "Where did they come from?"

The simple answer is "from living" just like all living organisms. Let me expand on that answer. I struggled with trying to conceptualize the inner working of the DID mind. I wanted to be able to explain it to my clients and other untrained people in terms everyone can understand. Was there something very different in their minds from what we call a normal mind? Right now, I'm not going into all the neurological literature. That is something you might want to explore for yourself.

There is plenty of it. If there was something very different about their minds, then we would have a real problem predicting just how they would function once they were of "ONE" mind. But I had witnessed, on more than one occasion, that once the barriers were removed they function just like typical human beings.

I ruled out the computer model because it couldn't explain their origin or guarantee continuity. However, it is helpful explaining current function remembering the "life line" concept where people can visualize their life as a "time line" from conception to death. Still something was missing. I marvel at the workings of the mind. When it's faced with a dilemma, it goes to work and comes up with a solution that turns out to be little more than common sense. The light bulb goes on, the moment of insight happens and oh yes! By superimposing 35 mm movie film over the life line we have a frame-by-frame record of every moment.

Those of you familiar with the hypnotic concept of age regression can easily see how this fits. Let me repeat my assertion that in almost every incident no formal induction is necessary since these folks are contently in a state of, at least mild, self-hypnosis and as such respond to any suggestion as if they were in a deep trance. This should simplify novice therapists' tasks and elevate their self-confidence to have successful outcomes without formal hypnotic training — not that it wouldn't be to their professional benefit to acquire hypnotic training for other reasons beyond working with DID clients.

I tend to digress, but I want this to be an easy read and simple to understand. That's not to insult my colleagues who are into more technical writings. In essence, I hope to take the reader, as my companion, on my journey to discovery.

Back to the 35 mm film. I imagine life as being a permanent record constantly recorded frame by frame on a continuously moving-forward 35 mm film with no chance of double exposure. Now, I realize this concept has its limits. ~~Portions~~ memory of the film ~~can be destroyed~~ or ~~damaged by disease, head trauma, hallucinations, dementi~~a and any number of things, including ~~false memories~~ superimposed by outside forces. Nevertheless, the film reference is about the best thing I came up with that seems to satisfy my clients and other rational minds. Unless there is structural change with the brain, life experiences recorded frame by frame are constant in their time frame. By rewinding the film to an earlier time it can only project what was recorded on it at that time, which is a factual account of that moment, assuming it hasn't been altered by anything or anybody.

Coalescence: This is the amalgamation of alters into one mind, the growing together of various alters. This is the actual "time healing all wounds." (Note: A client described what she saw inside her mind when I used the word coalescence as "*A cinderblock wall plastered over in various colors.*"

True Identity: This is only achieved after the final fusion has held for at least six months. During this time, the mind is coalescing and adaptive coping skills are acquired.

CHAPTER FIVE - THE CHALLENGE

It was widely held that:

E.L. Bliss wrote, "Abreactions are usually necessary" (Bliss, 1986, p. 212).

Colin A. Ross states, "… before two alters can integrate they must do a large amount of work" (Ross, 1989, p. 304).

Ross adds, "Clinical experience to date is that severely abused multiples must relive their trauma in a meaningful way in therapy in order to get better" (Ross, 1989, p. 251).

Richard Kluft, (1993) in presenting one of his "Ground Rules for the Treatment of MPD" concludes, "… what feeling has been buried must be abreacted… integration cannot be achieved without dealing with the impact of the past. The sense that the past has been dealt with and mastered is an essential aspect of the patient's recovery" (p. 95).

Bliss offers, "A challenge for the future is to find means to lessen them (abreactions) or to avoid them while still achieving therapeutic results…" (Bliss 1986, p. 212).

Bliss continues, the "therapeutic goal cannot be to expunge them (memories); rather it is to diminish the emotions that activate them… the painful past events, now contemporary, must be consciously assimilated, reconciled, rationalized and desensitized" (Bliss, 1986, p. 215).

As seen above, Bliss (1986) and Ross (1989) recognized the necessity of developing a successful technique to integrate which would diminish or preclude the use of abreaction, described by Kluft (1984) as *"surgery without anesthesia."*

Finally Colin A. Ross sums up the challenge, "... If someone could develop a method for treating multiple personality disorder that circumvented the abreactions, it would be wonderful" (Ross 1989, p. 248).

I leave it up to the reader to decide if the challenge has been met and the goal accomplished via the "As If" technique.

CHAPTER SIX - THE PROCESS

Introduction:

At a conference in early 1990, I was horrified as I watched a film by the presenter of a child alter abreacting. Immediately, I decided I could never bring myself to use abreaction as a pre-fusion therapeutic technique in working with multiples. Who am I to say, but it made no sense. How could a fractured ego state, with very limited life experience and coping skills, abreact and not simply be re-traumatized? Is this nothing more than revivification? The literature is full of case studies and journal articles in which the abreaction of buried feelings is presented as absolutely necessary and essential if lasting final integration/fusion is to be achieved (Bliss, 1986; Fike, 1990; Kluft, 1988, 1993; Putnam, 1989; Ross, 1988, 1989; Shapiro, 1001; Steel, 1989).

In working with individuals suffering from DID for the past 27 years, I gradually came to believe that negative affects could be effectively processed in a more intact ego system. To that end, I worked to join the most positive, and mature (e.g., those alters with the most positive life experience), alters first. My theory is, *"The larger the 'core' the easier it would be to process the negative affect encountered when the more abused/traumatized alters joined."* I visualized the trauma as sulfuric acid and theorized that a drop of acid released into the palm of one's hand would burn a hole in the hand. Drop that same amount of acid into a five-gallon bucket of water and you could drink it without being harmed. This technique does not bypass the traumatized event, for to do so would dilute one's life and in effect "kill off" an altered state of consciousness, as if that were even possible, without destroying parts of the brain. My promise to the "system" is, "*No life experience is lost!*" one of the biggest obstacles to alters, who view themselves as individuals, is they widely believe that by integrating they will die.

The problem with this initial technique was one may not totally escape the psychological effect (e.g., disappointment, sadness, regret, anger, shame, guilt, etc. associated with internal integrity) but could come pretty close to it. I reiterate the foregoing to emphasize that I believe Bliss (1986) is correct when he said, "The painful past events, now contemporary, must be consciously assimilated, reconciled, rationalized and desensitized." (p. 213). (Note: I realize I am taking Bliss out of context, in that he is referring to the after effects of abreaction). Bliss (1986) continues, the "therapeutic goal cannot be to expunge them (memories); rather it is to diminish the emotions that activate them" (p. 21).

It was at just one of those moments, while in the midst of fusing the 52nd alter (which held extremely painful life experiences) of a 42-year-old female, that the reoccurring question came into my mind, *"Isn't there a more humane way to facilitate the processing of traumatic experiences once the alter has fused with the core personality?"* (Note: As it ended up, the negative affect was removed almost simultaneously with the fusion of the alters during the 40-second "As If" ceremony.) Does it forever have to be as Richard Kluft, M.D. said, *"Surgery without anesthesia"*? (Kluft, 1984).

In a flash, the old adage, "time heals all wounds" popped into my mind. What would happen if, in fact, she was able to appropriate the effects of time in an instant, "As If" they had never been separate? For the answer to that question, I will let her speak for herself. See CHAPTER SEVEN "TRANSITIONAL CASE EXAMPLES." Case #1, "Caucasian middle-aged female with 137 alters."

To determine whether other therapists utilized similar treatment strategies, a review of the literature revealed a part of the technique. "As If" was first used by Adler (1956), and more recently by Carich (1991), to create "pseudo-time distortion: age progression and posthypnotic suggestion."

Then They Were One

One's mind is most creative while in the throes of a dilemma. At just such a time, while in the midst of an "As If" fusion ceremony, the thought came to me to say, *"Let time heal all wounds, remove all hurt, pain and suffering, process all life events from the time they happened to the present, as if they were never separate, freezing all hurt, pain and suffering, as it were, in a block of dry ice, causing that block of dry ice to turn into a vapor, go up into the air and then into outer space, never to return."* To my amazement, it worked!

All of the multiples were of the Christian faith. As such, they were very responsive to suggestions that corresponded to their belief system. Realizing that nature abhors a vacuum, I later added a benediction, "May the peace of God, which passes all understanding, fill the void left by the departure of the *hurt, pain and suffering.*" With these additions, this is basically the same process as "age progression to experience a positive future outcome." It allows the client to assimilate past life events, which would take an extended period of time with the use of abreaction, in only a fraction of that time. This is accomplished without revivification. The emphasis is on a "self-fulfilling prophecy."

(Note: As an afterthought, this is basically secular and can be used with anyone without a religious connotation.)

In referring to building a future orientation through the use of hypnotic age progression, Yapko (1988) writes,

"While the client experiences the age progression, the emphasis is on the experience of successful results based on changes actively made in one's behalf. Through the careful use of dissociation, the client can be temporarily dissociated from the effects of past experiences. In essence, this is accomplished indirectly since it is a future orientation that is amplified, relegating the past to a minor role at best in the process. Dissociation, whether in the temporal sphere or some other one, allows the clinician to amplify one dimension of experience in awareness and, in so doing, diminish others.

When the usual past orientation is minimized through the absorption of the individual in future possibilities and achievements, current choices (both conscious and unconscious) can be made in a way that is likely to bring them about. In essence, the clinician is facilitating the construction of a 'self-fulfilling prophecy.'

As a result, the client is able to experience a higher degree of confidence that current efforts are worthwhile, a positive source of motivation to continue on the path of recovery" (pp. 73, 74). (Note: Used with permission.)

Vaihinger, (1924) presenting the philosophy of "As If," states, "In the conditional clause something unreal or impossible is stated, and yet from this 'unreality' or impossible inferences are drawn. In spite of its unreality or impossibility, the assumption is still formally maintained. It is regarded as an apperceptive construct under which something can be subsumed and from which deduction can be made. What then, is contained in the 'as if'?

There must apparently be something else hidden in it apart from the unreality and impossibility of the assumption in the conditional sentence. These particles clearly also imply a decision to maintain the assumption 'formally, in spite of' these difficulties, between the 'as' and 'if', 'wie' and 'wenn', 'als' and 'comme' and 'si', 'qua-si', a whole sentence lies implied. What then, does it mean if we say that matter must be treated 'as if' it consisted of atoms? It can only mean that empirically given matter must be treated 'as' it would be treated 'if' it consisted of atoms or that the curve must be treated 'as' it would be 'if' it consisted of infinitesimals.... There is then, a clear statement of the 'necessity (possible or actuality) of an 'inclusion' under 'an impossible' or 'unreal assumption." (pp. 92, 93)

The "As If" ceremony from a Christian perspective

Since the original writing I have modified the "As If" ceremony. In almost all cases, I never initiate the ceremony until after I have gained permission from the core personality to join a specific alter (Note: For sake of identification I will call the core Linda and the alter Mary.)

After gaining Linda's permission to join, I said, *"Linda, close your eyes and just step inside to your right, but stay coconscious and listen to the conversation as I talk to Mary."*

Then I called the alter, using her name since she had one, *"Mary, come into the conscious mind."*

Thus done, I asked Mary, *"Are you ready to join?"*

I answered any questions Mary had and once she agreed to join I said, *"Go inside to your right but stay coconscious and see Linda."*

Now since they were always in some state of self-hypnosis, or highly suggestible state as you prefer, I only had to instruct them to: *"Turn and face each other. Linda (the core personality) reach out and take Mary's (the alter's) hands. Do you have them?"*

With a nod or a yes, I continued:

"Now as you embrace, we continue to form the core known as Linda. Let the pure white light, symbolizing God's blessing on this union, come down from heaven above, covering you from head to toe, both inside and out, permeating every part of your being, processing all life events from the time they happened until the present 'as if' you were never separate, causing all hurt, all pain, all suffering and all negative feelings to come out in the form of a vapor, forming a cloud above you, going up into the atmosphere, into outer space, never to return thus 'allowing time to have healed all wounds.'

Fill any void left by the departure of all the hurt, all the pain, all the suffering and all the negative feelings with the love and peace of God the Father, God the Son, and God the Holy Spirit that passes (or if you wish 'goes beyond') all understanding. Now, what God has joined together, let no one put asunder. (Note: I vary this at times and use 'let no one *take apart.*') *Now, as the light goes up, you open your eyes as Linda."*

Here's an interesting observation: Many clients with their eyes closed actually stretch out their arms, circle them as if embracing someone else and pull them in as the "As If" ceremony progresses, finally ending up hugging themselves. The distance they reached out is indicative of the alter's size.

A Secular variation of the "As If" Fusion Ceremony

(Note: This is not to devalue anyone in any way, shape or form. For all are given unconditional positive relief regardless of their beliefs.)

This is the "As If" ceremony a female client wrote after she had a very negative reaction to the above mentioned "As If" ceremony. It was a rather lengthy "As If" ceremony, much of which I was not comfortable incorporating in its entirety because it was untried.

After much reflection, I settled on the following version of the "As If" fusion ceremony which was successful in joining her alters. (Note: The names have been changed.) After gaining permission from the core, Jane, and the alter, Mary, I proceeded to administer the following ceremony:

I said, *"Jane, close your eyes and see Carol standing under the tree next to the lake.*

Walk over to her.

Jane, circle around Carol and face the west.

Carol, circle around Jane and face the east.
Join hands and circle slowly once around to your right as we continue to form the core we know as Jane.

Mother Earth is waking up the ground.

A green effervescent energy radiates up from the ground, covering you from head to toe, both inside and out.

Processing all life events from the time they happened until now, as if you were never separate.

Removing all hurt, pain and suffering causing it to come out in the form of a vapor, forming a cloud above your head, going up into the atmosphere, into outer space, never to return.

Allowing time to have healed all wounds.

As the effervescent energy returns to Mother Earth you will open your eye as Jane."

I have only used this version of the "As If" ceremony once. If I run into this problem again I would use my original "As If" ceremony which I will label the "Secular Version."

Variations leading up to the "As If" Ceremony:

1. If the alter is too young to understand, I tell the core, *"Walk over to the child/baby and reach down and take her/him by the hands. Pick her/him up. Embrace her/him."* Then I continue the "As If" ceremony by bringing down the light, etc. (Note: This has worked every time I've done it.)

2. If a very resistive alter has been put to sleep to keep her/him from sabotaging the therapy, on very rare occasions I have instructed the core to go over and take her/his hands and proceeded with the "As If" ceremony. (See CHAPTER TEN, ALTERS CREATING PROBLEMS, Case #7)

Earl Flora

CHAPTER SEVEN - TRANSITIONAL CASE EXAMPLES

Case #1: The first case is a middle-aged Caucasian female, married and a mother of three children who originally presented with 137 alters.

She wrote:

"It has decreased the amount of time it takes to join and integrate alter personalities in the core. This method eliminates the suffering and perceptual disturbances associated with joining alters together. In the past, I have endured the discovery and integration process of 43 alter personalities, each joining like a climax after a period of painful discovery.

What I experienced was like a gradual unfolding into my being. When other alters were joined into me, for a period of time their experiences were in a sense like a transparency laid upon me. If a child joined, my present perceptions were altered. I felt small. I was shocked to discover I had somehow grown breasts. Visual disturbances reoccurred, thought processes were slowed, and my ability for abstract thoughts was reduced. At times, I feared being abandoned like a child. In addition to altered perceptions, my children were like strangers to me. Even my husband became unfamiliar to me. On several occasions my sexual orientation has shifted and negatively affected the sexual responses to my husband.

As each new alter is integrated into me, my everyday life perceptions are changed. At times, my house has appeared alien to me. At other times, after joining, I have sat in my car fascinated by the lighted dials and felt too little to reach the pedals. Once, when I was joined with a younger alter, I was quite surprised that my husband had gray hair. I laughed every time I looked at him because he was so unfamiliar to me. I could not comprehend how he had gotten old instantly.

Earl Flora

Through my experience, it has become evident that the use of abreactions (by mental health professionals in joining alters) is totally unnecessary. It is not necessary to re-experience the pain in order to heal. One need not be burnt again to comprehend a past discomfort.

When I have seen (TV) documentaries on multiple personalities and the use of abreactions as a manner of treatment, it appears barbaric to me. Very caring professionals struggle through trial and error because there are little data as guidelines.

I can tell you from the other side of the coin because I am a multiple personality. My hope is that the mental health professionals will listen to me. Dr. Flora, whom I have been in therapy with for 12 months has developed a technique not utilized by other professionals working with multiple personalities. He does not believe in the use of abreactions. If great pain is present in an alter personality he takes the pain away and processes the experience separate from reliving the traumatic experience. He will go to an alter who can describe the events as an observer without re-experiencing the trauma.

There has been enough suffering. Why should one need to re-experience it? In a multiple, just because the core personality did not experience the trauma does not mean it was not experienced. All past trauma has already been experienced in some part by one or more alters. It is only necessary to bring that experience into the core. By joining an alter into the core personality a veil of energy is removed and the knowledge is absorbed. It is not necessary to relive trauma by the core personality.

By the use of this method of Dr. Flora's, I have been spared great suffering. It is my desire to proclaim to all the mental health professionals in an attempt to reduce the unnecessary suffering in integrating multiple personalities. Further, in Dr. Flora's work, he has made additional progress. About 40 percent of my discomfort has resulted after an alter personality has been integrated. The distortions in my perceptions have been inevitable. I have come to accept a period of adjustment after an alter is joined into me, (e.g., the core). The period of adjustment has not always been negative.

For example, my three children born from my body had separate mother alters. When the mothers of my first- and second-born children were joined into me, I gained the life experience and knowledge of me giving birth to them. They became more intimately my children."

(Follow-ups: Her final fusion of the 247th alter took place in 1998 and she has been dissociative-free ever since. You can read her testimony in CHAPTER FOURTEEN: TESTIMONIALS.)

Case # 2: She is a middle-aged, married, Caucasian female.
(Note: I had not used the new technique with any of her previous fusions.) After she had spontaneously fused the latest alter at home and gained knowledge of extremely painful memories, she attempted suicide by taking an overdose.

Fortunately, she was unsuccessful. I received a call from the emergency room doctor at 1 a.m. asking if I could come to the ER because they had done everything they could to revive her but to no avail. When I arrived they ushered me into her room. She was lying there with her eyes closed, apparently unresponsive. The doctor said her vital signs were almost normal, but she failed to respond to verbal cues. I tried calling her name several times. Tried talking to my internal co-therapist, tried talking to CT. Nothing was working.

Then, (Note: And please don't ask me how I come up with some of these ideas. They are not to be found anywhere except in this book!) I leaned over and whispered in her ear, "*If* (using the core's name) *you don't open your eyes and talk to me you are going to be taken to Eastern State Hospital*." (Note: Eastern State Hospital is the oldest psychiatric hospital in Virginia.) Well with that, her eyes opened! She looked up at me and said, "*Please don't put me in Eastern State Hospital*." The ER staff was dumbfounded. She was checked over and released at about 2 a.m. I then took her home and her the following afternoon in my office.

Earl Flora

She wrote:

"When I entered Dr. Flora's office, I still felt utterly hopeless. I just knew he would try to convince me that I wasn't as terrible as I believed I was. Maybe, he would tell me that he still liked me, which was the last thing I wanted to hear. Instead, he agreed with me, that I didn't deserve to live, but then no one did. (Note: As the core, she attended a Christian church. Therefore, I simply validated her convictions.) He then reminded me of God's mercy and love and how great that mercy is. That was why Jesus came and died were the only words I would allow myself to hear. Had Dr. Flora tried any other approach, he would have become completely discredited in my eyes. I knew what I had done and how I felt. No amount of justification about being separate or how the cult had maneuvered and tortured me into these acts would have made it acceptable or excusable.

Then Dr. Flora worked some real magic. With just a few words, he pushed the memories of what I had done into the past where they belonged."

(Note: Actually, no part of her did the deed, but she did not stop it either. In her separateness, the cult had programmed an alter to see what was happening as good rather than, as others outside the cult would see the act, as bad.)

By doing this, it allowed the healing power of time to take place in a matter of minutes.

She continued: "Now, less than 24 hours after leaving the hospital, I can recall all of these things and even write about them. Recalling these memories causes some pain and regret, but it isn't overwhelming. Now, I feel like all the pieces of the puzzle are in place. Now, I can take charge of my life rather than letting life just happen to me. We even discussed ways that I might be able to help others out of situations similar to what I had lived through."

(Follow-up: Shortly after this session she moved out of the state to escape the cult. Unfortunately, all contact was lost.)

Case #3: She is a Caucasian, mother of three children. She had never been in therapy before coming to me in 1990.

She said:

"Fusion has always seemed like a mixed blessing to me. While I really acknowledge that it is a vital positive step forward in the healing process, I have always found it to be painful, depressing and extremely difficult.

Immediately following fusion I have always experienced a loss of equilibrium, blurred vision, disorientation and confusion. The sudden introduction of traumatic memories has been devastating and overwhelming. I would find myself living and reliving the newly acquired memory and would be unable to focus on anything outside that experience. The newly fused parts of me fit like a lost piece of a jigsaw puzzle, but the connection felt uncomfortable somehow, like new shoes which are the right size and fit but don't really feel quite right for a while.

For several weeks, I would be very confused of the part of myself that had recently been someone else. I would frequently continue to call that part of myself by its former name, and although I knew, in detail, the things he/she had done while separate from me and could remember it, I often still felt a sort of alienation from my own self. The feeling of still having lines between the parts of myself often continued for a month or more.

The most difficult part of fusion for me, however, was the sudden introduction to emotions I had never experienced and did not know how to handle. In particular, rage and anger have been difficult. Several months ago, an alter was fused, who was nearly all rage. She felt betrayed and hurt and was furious at the world. I had no prior experience with that kind of fury and spent over a week trying to figure out what to do with it that would allow me to control the emotion rather than have it control me. After a while, the rage took its proper place in me and things settled down somewhat.

Earl Flora

Finally after several months, I felt that this negative emotion had some positive sides and could feel glad that it is in my arsenal of emotions.

Because of the difficulties I have experienced following fusion, I began to become increasingly reluctant to expose myself to the whole process. Then several weeks ago, Dr. Flora told me of the wonderful success he was having with some other people like me by using some new twists on the old fusion techniques. While I was happy for their positive experiences and their progress, I remained unconvinced that this was for me.

After some personal situations began to deteriorate directly due to our separateness, we, as a system, began to see that fusion was our only hope for survival. So, on Tuesday, 3/23/94, we decided to try again, in a big way. Prior to this day, we had not attempted to fuse any more than three alters in a single session and each of those fusions had been separate. On 3/23/94, an alter who wanted to fuse, but only if she could bring the 23 child alters, in her care, with her into the fusion. I told Dr. Flora that this is what we wanted, and he agreed.

After internal discussion, we decided that we wanted to be in circles with me, as the core alter, and the other adult alter in the center of two concentric circles, where all alters are touching and holding each other. The actual process of fusion was mostly the same, white light, the echoing voice, the sense that the only reality was inside the light, peace. The difference was that Dr. Flora directed each part to take its place as if the fracture had never happened and that the events and memories would be in their true place in time.

The barriers dropped, the light dimmed and what had been 24 alters was now, just me! I had no sense of dividing barriers, overwhelming emotional pain or any kind of physical discomfort. The events of 30 years ago were 30 years ago. I have not felt the compulsive need to re-examine each incident nor have I felt the flood of knowledge to be upsetting.

Immediately following this fusion, I felt a oneness with all of the parts of me. As if, we had never been separated and had always been me.

I am fully aware of the memories, but feel nothing more than regret for the people who hurt me having ever been so twisted as to do those things. Most of the time, I am not even aware of any difference in myself since this fusion, except that I now know more about who I am. This process has allowed me to regain my enthusiasm for therapy and healing and has left us anxiously waiting our next session where we can become me." (Lost contact after six months.)

Case # 4: "Abreaction and Me" by a 58-year-old widow.

She wrote:

"As long as I can remember, daily existing has been a huge struggle for me. Throughout my life, I was plagued with depression, (sometimes it would be very debilitating) and would also often alternate between bouts of high anxiety or emotional dormancy. Living life had become a pattern of dreading the hell of existing and wishing not to be alive or being distracted by obligations of having to get through the day. I frequently dealt with an exasperating difficulty of not remembering much of anything.

It seemed like I only operated in two modes, going from hyper-vigilance to moronic cluelessness. I felt like I was either incessantly arguing within myself or simply was too exhausted to pretend normalcy. I had never known what it felt like to be 'normal.' I felt that I was Humpty Dumpty, shattered into a million pieces, and Pinocchio, a wooden puppet with no hope of living as a real person. Needless to say, I could not bear to be me but coped with having to be on this earth by simply holding on for dear life with every fiber of my being and a deep resolve that I would not let the demons win.

Earl Flora

I can tell you that for the first 34 years of my life I did not acknowledge anything about what was going on inside of me except that I was maybe a little different. I was too busy trying to mimic everyone else's life. I had seen a therapist twice, for about six months apiece, but those sessions had just barely scratched the surface of my inner pain. The first round of sessions in 1988 addressed some of the physical violence that I had endured throughout my childhood. The second set of sessions in 1989 addressed the probability of sexual abuse that my mind had brought to light in the form of flashbacks but never actively remembered because of all the other traumatic experiences that I had suffered. Perhaps my subconscious was shielding me from further emotional disintegration and mental overload. I only know that I was an absolute, barely functioning mess.

I began a third round of therapy sessions with Dr. Flora around 1997. By then, I had retired from 20 years of military service and had reached the point of feeling completely and constantly tormented. Dr. Flora was listed as an abuse counselor and I decided to see someone because I realized once again that I was on the verge of losing it. He was gentle and seemed to understand that I was in great torment. However, I did not believe anybody could help me and became rather uncertain of the outcome when he talked about me having a dissociative disorder…or being of multiple personalities. I was going to college at the time for a degree (of all things) in psychology and was just beginning to understand the terminology as applied to the dynamics of life. Although I did not agree with his assessment, I could not ignore the presence of the uncontrollable dissociative influences and how they affected every aspect of being me. So I kept an open mind and paid close attention.

I had never been put into a hypnotic trance before in previous sessions. (Note: At this point I was not inducing a formal trance, simple instructing her to close her eyes. This is in essence a very light trance as demonstrated by her following description of the session.) What got my attention initially are the things that came out of my mouth and the emotional content that accompanied whatever surfaced while under the influence of hypnosis.

Then They Were One

I was always fully aware of everything while in this relaxed state and was able to discuss each experience immediately afterwards and we simply explored whatever was in my head. I felt some relief because I began to realize that maybe I was not nuts, just very wounded, and it was cathartic to just talk about some of the deep dark secrets that I thought no one else would believe or ever understand. I did learn to look forward to the hypnotic sessions because they offered internal relief, unusual insight and uncensored memory bites, complete with concentrated bursts of whatever emotion accompanied the recollection at that time.

Unfortunately, time was limited. The companies began to fight with each other. We were notified that the coverage would be terminated in two weeks. Dr. Flora was more aware than I was about the ramifications of losing counseling capabilities. I was not in an emotionally stable frame of mind but I had developed an intricate defense system that filtered everything and had enabled me to survive this far. He knew that I was strong and stubborn. I clung to survival by sheer will even though I was so very vulnerable. I did not know it at the time, but looking back, I believe that God had a hand in our decision to do what Dr. Flora called an emergency fusion. We discussed the 'procedure' and I requested that he do whatever it took to bring me relief.

If I did not believe in dissociative disorders before, what I experienced, once Dr. Flora performed the fusion of parts into me, convinced me that there was some validity to his assessment. He put me in a hypnotic state, simply talked to my subconscious and told my parts to join. I am sure he did this in a fancier way than I am stating, but I was too busy concentrating on what was going on to remember his words.

At first, I thought he had lost his mind and this was just a waste of time. However, within 24 hours I was in the throes of the best and worst emotional roller coaster ride of my adult life. I awoke the next morning and began to relive every traumatic incident of my young life, with my adopted family.

Earl Flora

There is a difference between remembering and reliving. One is controlled in memory bites and the other is equivalent to being transported back in time, complete with all the emotional content of the experience as well. I believe that is much the same as experiencing Post-Traumatic Stress Disorder. Not only could I not function, I was in a type of emotional labor, complete with serious pain.

As I drifted from memory capsule to memory capsule, I felt each trauma as if it was almost real time. And there were a lot of capsules. It seemed like a never-ending involuntary parade of trips down memory lane, each one feeling something intense but different. I will also add that I was not sure which was worse, experiencing it the first time or reliving it the second time. I was incapable of functioning, period. I believe my husband called the doctor and he gave the command over the phone to cease the fusion. The next week, he explained the abreaction, or flooding as it is now called.

The following is an excerpt from my journal that was written after the first fusion on March 29, 1998:"

"I have so much to say but don't want to write it because I don't like what I have to write. This weekend has been amazing. One must go through it to truly understand. I know I didn't have a clue beforehand. I believe I have just uncovered the tip of the iceberg. Friday when it started to happen I knew I was going down for the count. But wasn't sure how far down. I have felt great pain in my life but that (this) pain was unique. It was like giving birth or taking a big dump after a long period of constipation. It literally erupted within and they rocked me with wave after wave of emotions. I was helpless, weak and within its power. There was no energy to fight or even want to fight. I spoke things — whatever came to my head. I felt fear, death, anxiety, great sadness, loneliness, bitterness, dirty, shamed, violated, disgust and hurt. There were probably other things in there but I had no strength to sort them anymore. I looked for anger and couldn't find any room left or energy to even deal with anger.

Then They Were One

Throughout all this I was a captive but willing. Now I rejoice because what I feel, even if it is painful is mine, all mine!

Saturday, I had class all day and I was worried about surviving it. But I woke up feeling alive — something I hadn't felt in a long time. I was fine in class, but had noticed that when I slowed down the things come a-knocking and I have to deal with them. They still feel awful. They stir up great panic inside me. I want to run and hide. I won't let Bill (Note: Not real husband's name.) leave me because of that. But there is also the side that cherished every little thing in wonderment. That is there too and I don't want lose that.

I don't sleep well. Nightmares all the time, but I don't wake up scared. I seem to understand somehow.

My mind thinks like a child sometimes. OK, a lot! This child wants to be a child. She knows she is out of whack but demands her time. I suppose in my private moments I will give it to her. I don't mind showing Bill the child but my children don't need this side of their mother.

There is a definite line between life and existence. I had existed for the last several years. Now I want to live. I know there is a lot more to be done but feel we can do it. The only trouble is that it is hard to be a kid when you have to be a parent. I want time to go thru this but don't think it is possible.

I had to take a shower Friday night because I felt the definite need to wash it all off me. That was weird, that and the constant adrenalin rush to my head even in the weakest of conditions. I was drained but not physically tired. ~~*I could not move but only because I was being held down by my emotions.*~~

'I think I want to throw a temper tantrum.'

Earl Flora

While I may have suffered due to the earlier fusion, it served a huge purpose. I finally realized that it was not my fault that I was the way I was. I consistently blamed myself for not being able to overcome my past and was convinced that I was nuts. If I had discussed what was going on to make me behave so bizarrely, many a well-meaning person had responded with 'well that is in the past' or 'you just need to move on.' I began to accept that this was done to me and was nothing that I could just wish away. What I had to do was learn, pay attention and not give up. I also realized that maybe Dr. Flora was more knowledgeable than me and I should keep an open mind.

Time ran out on allotted insurance visits and we could not financially afford to subsidize them on our own.

My husband died from a tragic accident in July of 2011. Our children were grown up and out of the house for the most part. We had become members of a local church and I was still struggling. In the past 12 years I had attempted to make many strides toward feeling 'normal' but never succeeded. I attributed my failure to feel better as my fault and was aware that I was on a downward spiral. I was helpless to stop the process. I had finally learned to believe in God, and love him but did not believe that God loved me because I was bad.

My husband and I would talk a lot but nothing could convince me otherwise. It was not long after his death that I drove myself back to Dr. Flora. I had lost my husband's group insurance due to his death. With my new insurance, I realized it was possible to return to the only therapist that had seemed to make a difference. Once again, there was nothing left to hold on to and I felt like I was losing it. The pain and torment were overwhelming, unabated because I was all alone. There just happened to be a cancellation that very hour and it was mentioned by his office manager that it was an act of God.

Dr. Flora resumed his fusion, or joining techniques, but this time he had perfected it and added a process of giving it to God and taking out the hurt, the pain and the suffering. I did not comprehend it all at first, but as time went on, my burden of living got a bit lighter. I began to actively help him piece together many parts or encapsulations of my past. I began to understand the mechanics of my intricate defense mechanisms, the depth of my brainwashing and the debilitating effect it had on daily living. I understood that I was still a prisoner of my past and only God, this therapy and hard work on my part would be able to free me. I would have accepted just being free from pain, but what I got was so much more.

I learned that my subconscious had encapsulated my traumas because I could not deal with them as real-time memories. If you have as many traumas as I had that were affecting my heart and head, then you can imagine the torment that I was experiencing. Dr. Flora extracted each capsule and painstakingly joined them one at a time in such a way that it was able to be processed.

It was not fun to recall these traumas. However, not only did his process work but it was less traumatic, much more endurable and little by little I began to think, function, become less reactive to daily living and even began to feel some emotions. That was really a neat experience because I had spent all of my life not feeling much but processing everything through a series of logical thoughts built by my defense mechanisms. I learned that one cannot deal with what needs to be dealt with unless you can actually access the problem. When they are shielded by layers of filters the healing cannot begin. Actually facing the difficulty (I call it rolling around in the ditches) is a necessary step toward healing.

It has been three years now and I am almost done. More importantly, I actually feel that Humpty Dumpty has been superglued together and Pinocchio was allowed to become a real boy. I used to be a strange version of a 'basket case,' but now embrace my differences and try to channel them toward living in God's will. I cannot help but believe that the hand of God has been on me the entire time. I simply had to open my heart and mind enough to understand, actively seek help and *never give up.*

Earl Flora

I had to find the strength to not try to do this alone, but learn to trust God first and then Dr. Flora a little bit at a time.

I can honestly say that I believe God led me to Dr. Flora because I was supposed to understand the rest of the mechanics it takes to heal. In turn, I hope to encourage others who endure unbearable suffering to seek first the God who can do *all* things and trust that He will lead you to where you need to be. At 58 years old, to be free from constant torment is something I never thought would be in my realm of possibility. To learn how to enjoy life and look forward to living each day is nothing short of a miracle. To have the opportunity to minister to others in hopes that they too will feel the joy in living is an honor and privilege.

Post note: She continues in Post Fusion Therapy and has just married her sweetheart.

CHAPTER EIGHT – DISCUSSION - RESISTANCE TO CHANGE

During the past 27-plus years I have worked with well over 100 clients with DID. Much to my sadness, the majority of them dropped out of therapy for one reason or another. I suspect that I moved too quickly, failed to win their confidence or overcome their resistance, or just plain missed some important elements that could have helped them stay the course and completely integrate their lives. Since dissociation is a primary defense mechanism, convincing those whose system utilized dissociation almost exclusively that there is a better way is not a simple task. After all, the system believes it cannot survive without it, for without it all the hidden memories would become conscious and that would mean that the system would die. Others have told me they are not interested in finding out what happened since it is hidden.

I rather suspect the real truth is they are afraid of what they will discover, and I might add, I fully understand. As the therapist I too am hoping that what is hidden is not of such a nature that it could have the direst consequences if brought to light. So far, there has been only "ONE" case that almost cost her life once the memory was acquired. Fortunately that was one of the cases mentioned earlier which had a positive outcome. Who is to say the next client might not be the one with a past that could be devastating. Then there is that "well-meaning" protector alter, whether interject or not, who stands in the way by blocking other alters from participating in the therapy. Most of the time it takes extra time to win him/her over and just allow the others to make up their own minds.

Currently I am treating six clients diagnosed with DID. They are all making significant progress in integrating their lives "without abreaction. They have been spared the pain of abreaction as described in the four case examples.

Earl Flora

CHAPTER NINE - SPECIAL TECHNIQUES

Interjects, aka pseudo alters

A variation of the "As If" technique works on interjects as well. As stated above, interjects are what appear to be regular alters created by the process known as dissociation. In most cases, they were inserted by someone outside of the body or internally by deliberate subconscious force. No matter which way they were created, they were deliberately brought into the mind for a specific purpose. There repertoire is limited in scope. They are the figment of either outside or internal imaginations. As such they are not the result of compartmentalized traumatic life experiences (e.g., alters, altered states of consciousness or alter personalities).

Cult induced interjects

Cults have injected personas for control. A satanic cult injected me into the mind of a multiple as a cult member. She told me we engaged in sexual activity. This was their way of discrediting me with my client. (Note: It did not work, because I asked CT to tell her the truth.)

In some cases, the subconscious mind itself brought them into the system in their entirety (e.g., living, dead, abusive, hateful parents or relatives). At first glance, they will appear just like all the rest, but under further investigation, you will begin to see subtle differences. Since they are not natural alters, in most cases, they do not have a life, in the conscious mind, in the same way natural alters do, how be it, in a limited sense.

Knowing my theological background, a male satanic cult interject (Note: I believe he was the one who had the gun and was ordered to kill me.) challenged me to several theological debates, namely, *"What was the big deal with them sacrificing several black cats on Halloween when God killed His son, Jesus, on the cross?"* In spite of limited conscious experience, as an interject, I was never able to fuse him.

Earl Flora

Ultimately he had to be removed by reversing the process that injected him into the mind in the first place.

To protect the client's identity I will provide no demographics and will call her Betty. For some time, Betty's malevolent mother, father, grandfather and nephew appeared to be alters. In addition, other relatives, such as her sister, appeared to be alters.

For several months, before it was established they were interjects, I tried to reason with them, as I do with all alters, especially if I knew they came into being when the body was of adult age. (Note: Just a reminder, I always ask the alters, when they are first identified, to tell me what they hear inside their head when I ask, "*How old are you now*?" Once I have that age I ask, "*How old was the body when you were born*?") Needless to say, I was becoming frustrated with the lack of progress. Nothing I tried worked!

The mother tried to intimidate me by calling me, among other things, a quack. Internally, she would repeatedly tell her daughter, "*Nobody loves you. You're better off dead*," telling her to take her medications all at once and die. This resulted in several hospitalizations for apparent suicide attempts.

I tried to block the inner voices by suggesting that Betty could not hear them. That worked for a few days, but the voices returned. I moved the voices so far back from Betty that she could not hear them, only to have the voices return by the next session. I gave Betty an internal volume control to reduce the sound of the voices. This worked for a short time. I finally placed the voices in a sound-proof room with no doors and no windows but, CT told me, they tunneled out under the wall and continued their relentless tirade.

I tried reasoning with them to stop or they would force me to have them feel the pain Betty endured as the result of their suggestions. This also worked for a short interval. I attempted cognitive restructuring, filling them with love instead of hate. This actually lasted longer than anything previously tried.

The mother was aware something had changed in her, but she was not certain just what. It took only two weeks and she was back to her old tricks. By that time, I was very frustrated and running out of options.

As this was early on in the evolution of my "As If" technique, I could not understand why techniques I used successfully before, with other clients, were not working in Betty's case. I began to wonder, just what was I up against? If they were normal alters, why didn't they respond to my suggestions?

This led me to begin considering the possibility that something was very different about them. I began to entertain the idea that they were not your average alters.

If they were not average alters, then what could they be? Who and what were they and how did they get into Betty's mind? Remembering that the birth mother was involved in the satanic cult during Betty's early life, I began to reason it might be some form of re-embodiment or spirit possession.

I searched the web for information on re-embodiment and/or spirit possession. I was aware of several Biblical accounts of spirit/demon possession, but these did not fit this profile. The trail led back to only one conclusion, as Sherlock Holms was wont to say to Dr. Watson, "Elementary, my dear Watson." They must be interjects! As interjects, they could never be fused/integrated into the core system. They would have to be removed completely from the inner world as figments of the imagination. This was accomplished by the *Reverse Installation* technique previously described in the CHAPTER FOUR on DEFINITIONS.

Therapist-induced interject

Question: "When is it ever therapeutic for the therapist to interject him/herself into a client?"

This may come as a surprise to some of my colleagues, but therapists may accidentally or purposefully inject themselves into the system.

Situation:

This situation is about a client we'll call Mildred who was heavily involved in the satanic cult. She disappeared after attending her last session the night before. Her husband could not find her. When I arrived at my office the next morning I found her sitting in her car in a comatose-like trance. With some effort I got her out of her car while she was still in a trance. I was able to bring her out of the trance but she would not respond to me when I called her name.

I called out CT, who informed me they were told the cult had killed me last night. I asked where Mildred was and was informed the cult had turned her into stone the night before. All my efforts to bring her into the conscious mind failed. I had never before done what follows, but in that moment, I decided to inject myself into her psyche.

In essence I said, "*On the count of three, I will be inside where Mildred is turned into stone, one, two three. I am breathing the breath of life into your body* (Note: A version of CPR). *As I do, all barriers that keep you from coming out are beginning to erode.*"

In a very short period of time, Mildred opened her eyes and screamed, "*You are alive!*" She continued, "*I remember leaving* (name deleted) *house* (last night) *turning the corner. Then nothing until I was in this room.*"

From her perspective, once she opened her eyes I was back in my office chair talking with her.

Exorcism: Demon possession

Caution: This is not for everybody to try. Refer any such cases to a member of the clergy that feels qualified to perform an exorcism.

In working with a client who was strongly influenced by the satanic cult, after all the interjects were removed there remained this, what for a better name, I will refer to as an "entity." CT described it as, *"smelling like shit!"*

In consultation with another minister, it was decided this entity was probably a demon of sorts, not a cult-induced interject. He agreed to be in the session in which, after he deferred to me, I was to perform an exorcism.

As an ordained Southern Baptist minister, as well as a clinical psychologist, I am fully cognoscente of the words Jesus used as He cast out the unclean spirits as recorded in the book of Mark 1: 23-25 (King James Version). "…. a man with an unclean spirit. And he cried out, saying, 'Let us alone; what have we to do with thee, Jesus of Nazareth? Art thou come to destroy us? I know thou art the Holy One of God.' And Jesus rebuked him, saying 'Hold your peace and come out of him.' And when the unclean spirit had torn him, and cried in a loud voice, he came out of him."

We received the authority to cast out devils in the book of Mark 16:17 (King James Version). Jesus says, "These signs shall follow them that believe; in my name (Jesus) shall they cast out devils …"

My client consented to the exorcism. (Note: As I write this from my session notes, it has been so long ago that I cannot remember every unwritten detail, but I'm positive I would not have attempted this without a lot of prayer for God's guidance and help.) With her seated opposite me, with her eyes closed, in a firm, confident, somewhat authoritarian tone I began:

"In the name of Jesus Christ, the Son of the living God, I rebuke you demon, that smells like shit, to come out from (name removed) and the slime pit and any other place within her system and enter into the bowels of the earth. Fill any void left with the love and peace of God that passes all understanding. I entreat thee Holy Spirit, the Restrainer of evil, to surround her and protect her from the forces of Satan!"

In order to be sure the demon was gone, I invoked the command five times adding the Trinity for good measure. I told the demon in a commanding tone, "*In the name of Jesus Christ, God almighty and the Holy Spirit depart!*" She jerked and went limp. She hugged herself and grimaced. She came around and began to reorient herself.

I asked, "*What was your internal impression surrounding the exorcism?*"

At first she said, "*I was afraid you were tricking me!*"

Followed by, "*We just had a big earthquake.*"

(Note: It was put into the earth!)

Other than what I have written above, I have no other evidence there was a bona fide demon exorcised and not a satanic-cult interject. The fact remains whatever it was, it was gone after the exorcism. You be the judge.

A word of caution

Many well-meaning Christians and other faiths see DID as a form of demon possession. My approach is to see if any malevolent alters remain that have not responded to the various techniques employed to effect final integration. Then and only when it becomes evident there is a genuine demon would I attempt another exorcism or refer my client out to a member of the clergy with experience performing exorcisms.

Example of a church-sponsored exorcism with a DID

Years ago, while attending a conference on MPD, the speaker, who was herself a Multiple Personality, described how the church she attended insisted she was demon possessed. The pastor talked her into allowing him to perform an exorcism to free her body of this demon. Internally, she knew she was not demon possessed, but now she had agreed to the exorcism. So what to do?

Remember my earlier observation about these folks being highly intelligent and, I might add, ingenious. (Note: That is one of the reasons I love working with them.) The old adage says, "*The essence of genius is simplicity.*" (Author unknown.) So the subconscious mind created its own interject to be the demon that was going to be exorcised. It worked! The church was proud it exorcised the demon and the system was relieved to stop hearing she was demon-possessed. I guess you could call this a win-win situation if it wasn't for the subterfuge.

My first encounter with a "demon" or so he said

The very first MP female I encountered suddenly switched from a very soft female voice to an evil-sounding, raspy, threatening tone screaming at me to back off and leave her alone. He identified himself as the demon who was there to protect her from any threat. It was obvious the demon considered me a threat by his very intimidating tone. To deny I was frightened would be a lie. At first I was startled, shaken and the hair stood up on the back of my neck! I was frightened and uncertain as to what course of action to take.

My first instinct was to follow his instructions and move away from her and stop trying to help. However, I stood my ground and engaged him in dialogue. Again my theological education provided me with the right question to ask. As mentioned in the book of James 2:19 (Amplified Bible), James writes, "*You believe that God is ONE, you do well. So do the demons believe and shudder* (in terror and horror such as make a man's hair stand on end and contract the surface of his skin.)" (Note: That pretty well describes my reaction to meeting a so-called "demon.")

So, knowing demons believed in the Deity of Jesus, I asked this demon, "*Is Jesus the Son of God?*" In the same gravelly voice he answered a definite "*No!*" With that reply the hair on the back of my neck settled down and I quickly regained my composure, calmed down and knew without a shadow of doubt that he was not a satanic demon.

Homicidal alters, not interjects

These alters believe if they could just get rid of a certain alter or alters everything would be just fine. I first try to engage them in a dialogue to determine specifically why they feel the way they do. I reassure them that I'm sympathetic to their plight, but there is just one very serious problem with their plan.

I ask them, *"Are you planning to commit suicide?"*

They will inevitably answer in the negative like, *"Do you think I'm crazy?"*

Once I have their attention, I ask, *"Are you aware I have promised to always tell the truth?"*

Once I get an affirmative answer, I say, *"This is going to be hard for you to believe since you see yourself as separate and not a part of their body. What do you think will happen to you if you kill them or encourage them to commit suicide or drive the car off the road while you are riding in it?"*

They almost always answer, *"Nothing."*

I continue, *"Well, this may come as a great shock to you, but since you share the same body, you will in truth be committing mass murder and suicide and die with all the rest of those you see inside."*

He/she will deny the truth of that statement. So, I say, *"I'm looking at you and I see the exact body clothed in the exact clothes as they are."*

Don't expect them to instantly agree with you, because the truth is so far from their perspective that if I were them, I wouldn't believe it either. However, this is the beginning of knowledge not the end.

It is more likely the threat is real and will continue at this stage of the therapy. So I have a couple of options if I'm going to be able to keep them alive:

(1) I attempt to acquire a commitment that no one will try to kill themselves, others or encourage others to commit suicide or murder, be it by direct action or by suggestion. In addition, I secure my CT's promise to call me if there is a real threat.

(2) If that fails, I ask them if they would like to go to Disneyland or some exotic destination of their choice for the duration, at my expense. I tell them they cannot return until I send for them. I have done this successfully on more than one occasion and it works. The threat disappears with them. After much work and after most of the alters joined the core, I bring them back (Note: I keep a running list of the alters on the inside of manila folders and put a date by the names when they join. This way I don't forget who is where. That can be embarrassing.). Usually, by then I can convince them to at least agree to a trial fusion or an out-and-out fusion. Of course the emotional, traumatic reason for the threat was removed during the "As If" ceremony and the core quickly assimilated the alter without becoming suicidal or homicidal.

(3) The third and least-preferred solution is to actually block them by locking them up in a place where they cannot get out and cannot be heard by the others. After most of the alters have joined the core, I will bring them out one at a time and work at gaining their trust, by reassuring them their life experience is invaluable for the survival of the entire system. This can be a lengthy process. It is not something that should be rushed, as long as I can be assured they cannot harm themselves or others. No small part of the process is to get the core to agree to accept alters who in the past have been anything but "persona non grata," to say the least.

Keeping in mind, final fusion is the goal, invite them to take their place in the core where they will have a part in the decision-making process. (Note: It has been my experience the most violent alters are actually interjects and do not respond to therapists as do the natural alters. In that case initiating the "Reverse Installation" process, in effect, erases them from the mind since they were actually "pure imagination" in the first place.)

Closely related trauma

Four alters ranging in age from 8 to 21 years old who were traumatized by events that left them feeling unwanted, abandoned and friendless agree to be joined together. I had them form a circle by holding hands. Next I placed the core in the center of the circle. Then, I had them, while holding hands, slowly tighten up the circle and move in to make contact with the core. I had the core put her arms around them and had them embrace her. Then I simply conducted the "As If" fusion ceremony and they all joined simultaneously.

An alternative method that works just fine is to join them one at a time and ask for feedback to be certain the core has assimilated the history. Then repeat the process until all that wanted to join are joined.

ALTERS REFUSING TO JOIN THE CORE

A little background is needed at this point:

Historically, therapists would bring the traumatized alters out and have them abreact, re-experiencing the painful trauma in order to be desensitized. Through this process the amnestic barriers were removed. I believe, as with others, the reason for the barriers in the first place was *not the event itself* rather it was *the negative affective response* that caused the separation.

So, as already stated, I completely reject abreaction and instead utilize the non-re-traumatizing *"As If, they were never separate, thus allowing time to heal all wounds, removing all pain, all suffering, all anger and all negative feelings having it come out in the form of a vapor above their heads, going up into the atmosphere and outer space, never to return, etc."*

When I'm faced with a refusal, I do not force alters to join. *"So the question is: How can I remove the amnestic barriers without going through the entire "As If" ceremony and not violate their discretion?"*

The thought came to me: *"What would happen if I removed the negative affect without joining them? If the reason for the separation was removed would they not naturally come together, over time, since the system was no longer threatened by the negative affect and still not violate the free will?"*

Example One: A partial "As If" fusion ceremony

That's what I did with an alter who refused to join. I removed the negative affect by abbreviating the "As If" ceremony. I asked my client to close her eyes and observe what is going to happen. I said, *"Let the pure white light come down from heaven above covering Debby from head to toe, permeating every part of her body, both inside and out, processing all life events for the time they happened to the present as if they were never separate, causing all hurt, all pain and all suffering to come out of her in the form of a vapor, thus allowing time to have healed all wounds, going up over her head into the atmosphere, into outer space never to return. Fill any void left by the departure of the hurt, pain and suffering with the love and peace of God the Father, God the Son and God the Holy Spirit."* My client reported seeing the little girl go over into a corner, lie down, curl up and go to sleep.

A few sessions later the young alter was awakened and once again asked if she wanted to join. Without hesitation, she agreed and the fusion was successfully affected. However, she did not spontaneously join. I can only speculate that could have been because she stayed asleep and was not embraced with the core.

Example Two: A little girl kept moving out of reach

A client who had joined what appeared to be the last alter continued to experience great difficulty joining in and/or participating in various church activities. These were namely those that required her to repeat various sayings like "God loves you and so do I."

This description came out after I had asked her to repeat, *"If it is to be, it's up to me!"* She barely repeated it and then refused to do so again, describing an internal resistance but not verbal. I asked her to just close her eyes and tell me what she sees as I said, *"The one who is causing this resistance materialize."*

She said, *"It's a young girl."*

I asked CT, *"How old was she when she was born?"* My client reported hearing three.

I asked, *"What is the girl doing?"*

She said, *"She is just sitting alone."*

I asked my client to approach her. She reported the girl repeatedly moved just out of her reach as she attempted to get close enough to take her hand.

I decided to say, *"Bring the white light down and cover the little girl, instantly removing all the hurt, pain and suffering, causing it to come out in the form of a vapor, causing it to go up into the atmosphere and outer space never to return again. Fill any void left by the departure of the hurt, pain, and suffering with the love of God that passes all understanding. As the light goes up, open your eyes."*
I asked my client, *"What did you witness?"*

Then They Were One

She surprised me by saying *"She's in my arms!"*

So I continued to administer the "As If" fusion ceremony and they were joined together. This partially supported my theory of a spontaneous fusion. It certainly caused her to be amenable to joining and she did.

Observation: Dissociation is the result of negative affect.

I cannot say it enough, the foregoing confirmed the hypothesis, shared by many professionals, that dissociation is not the rejection of the event, rather the rejection of the negative affect associated with the event. Thus, by removing the negative affect, the hurt, pain and suffering that caused the event to become compartmentalized into an altered state of consciousness in the first place no longer needed to remain separate. With the negative affect eliminated, it no longer threatens the system. As such, the life event/experience spontaneously integrates.

Let me add, integration is only instantaneous when two or more alters are fused. Full integration of the combined life experiences will coalesce over time. It is like breaking down an interior wall in your home. Once it is gone the area is expanded. What were two rooms instantly become one larger room. So with the walls removed, over time, one will automatically adjust to the expanded area. That is what my clients have repeatedly told me happens to their combined life experience.

Forgive me if I repeat myself at times, but I want to make it clear to those who are not familiar with working with this population, their minds do not homogenize like mixing various colors of paint, but rather the life events remain in chronological order. Their personality styles, interests, talents, family, friends, work, intellect, etc., no longer compete but rather complement. This becomes the repertoire that can now be drawn upon as a source of wisdom in making current choices, as well as long-term plans for the greater good of the emerging individual.

Earl Flora

A word of encouragement, "I'm tired of being alone, I'm ready."

Not to worry! An old nursery rhyme, about obstinate sheep, comes to mind: *"Leave them alone and they will come home wagging their tails behind them."*

If I might be allowed to sum it up in a paraphrase, I have been told, by more than one hold-out alter, words to this effect, *"It's pretty lonely inside here with no one to talk to, so what the heck. I'm tired of being alone. I'm ready."* Then with no hesitation in "60 or less seconds," the fusion is accomplished.

CHAPTER TEN - ALTERS CREATING PROBLEMS

Case #1

PROBLEM: Geriatric male suddenly regresses to early childlike behaviors

Process:

An elderly Caucasian male with no prior history of DID began to exhibit childlike regressive behavior (e.g., bouncing from one wall to another, tapping his fingers obsessively, flailing his arms, rubbing his legs and imitating an Indian-like war dance), all out of his control.

After his psychiatrist ruled out medical and medication side effects, I challenged him, once again, as to whether he was hearing voices or his thoughts out loud in his head. He paused for several seconds and answered, *"No."*

I asked him, *"If a person is hearing his or her thoughts out loud what would that indicate?"*

He answered, *"They would be crazy!"*

I explained, for the umpteenth time, that it depended on whether the voices would talk to him in the third person as well as talk to me. Then I told him to tell me if he heard an answer inside his head when I asked his subconscious mind a question. He agreed. With that I asked, *"Subconscious, do you understand what I'm saying?"*

He reported hearing, *"Yes."*

With that I said, *"Close his eyes and look inside your mind. Tell me what you see after I instruct your CT to show you who is causing all these movements."*

I said, "*CT, please show him who is causing all these movements.*"

He said, "*It's a little boy alone in his room in his crib, yelling and screaming and bouncing around from one side to the other.*"

I said, "*CT, tell him to tell you how old he is.*"

He reported hearing *"three."*

Since the session was almost over I decided to simply say, "*On the count of three, the 3-year-old boy will fall fast asleep until the next session.*"

The man reported instantly seeing him fast asleep in his crib. Then I asked him, "*What was it like for you to actually see yourself at age 3?*"

He was almost speechless, but managed to say, "*It was something!*"

Finally, after many attempts to develop a rapport failed, I referred him to a neurologist, since he was not responding to my efforts, to rule out organic brain damage. Unfortunately at that point, he dropped out of therapy with the psychiatrist and me.

Case #2

PROBLEM: Shoplifting joke backfires

Process:

In this case, two malevolent alters decided to play a trick on the primary personality that ended up with the primary personality being arrested, charged with a felony and given jail time.

Then They Were One

I was able to find out what happened by simply asking for anybody that knew what happened to come and tell me about it. A male alter admitted he took over as they approached the checkout counter and proceeded to push the shopping cart right past the counter and store manager and out the front door. Then the male alter went back inside as the store manager tapped the primary persona on the shoulder. She had no idea what happened as she had the money and intended to pay for the items. Instead she was arrested. The male alter blamed the idea on a malevolent female alter whose sole purpose was to punish the primary personality for past wrongs.

After I explained to both of them that they will probably spend time in jail as the result of their actions, they agreed to come out in court and testify. Even though it's not my favorite thing to do, I agreed to appear in court, on her behalf, at the sentencing phase of the trial.

I was able to bring both alters out. They testified in open court, but to no avail as the judge sentenced them to four months in jail. After their release, I referred them to the local Community Service Board across the street from their residence because of too many missed appointments blamed on transportation problems.

In addition, after their release, there was little or no interest in resolving their separateness.

(Note: once again, the courts view DID defendants as one person. The judge commented that all three sounded just alike. I explained that was because all three were adults. I asked the judge if he wanted me to bring out a child alter so he could hear a different voice. He declined. This is not to fault the judge, as he is not in the mental health field, but only to highlight the difficulty the legal system faces when dealing with DID. Actually in every case, the issue of the defendant's DID diagnosis was given fair hearing.)

Earl Flora

Case #3

PROBLEM: Whether to join a sleeping alter

Process:

In this case, a male in his early twenties suddenly dissociated after we had joined what we thought was the last alter. In other words, a new alter was able to manifest himself as the result of the amnestic barrier coming down. Later it was discovered he had been the product of a reaction to his parents arguing loudly with each other. The problem was he liked to spend money in the bar drinking, drugging and hitting on the female bartender. The problem was he would then drive home drunk. He was totally against merging with the core.

Since we were at the end of the session, I decided he was not going to modify his behavior, so I simply put him to sleep in order to protect the whole system. He was still asleep six weeks later when my client returned after working out of town for a month.

How, you ask, can you accomplish that? Well, it is as simple as saying, "On the count of three, you will fall into a restful sleep and will stay asleep until I wake you up."

So here we are six weeks later and he is still asleep. My client is employed full time, in a new job where he is moving up the ladder quickly. The problem is periodic drug screening. What was I going to do about the spice–loving, sleeping alter who had refused to even consider a trial fusion? I do not like to be duplicitous while working with these folks. It can come back later and interfere with the therapy.

I considered waking him up. However, I was afraid I could not control him. Forcing him to join was not an option. After much discussion including the core personality and the subconscious, it was decided to join him while he was asleep.

Since this would be a first, I decided to have the core close his eyes and approach the sleeping alter. (Note: even though his eyes are closed, they are open on the inside. Open eyes are implied by saying, "*Tell me what you see.*) He reported he was standing next to the sleeping alter. I told him, "*Take one of his hands*. (Note: This is a technique in which the life experiences can be transferred from one alter to another alter by simply suggesting it will happen.) *When you do you will instantly know what he did while he was in the conscious mind.*"

The core wanted to join him, so without awakening the alter, I instructed the core to take him by both hands and embrace him. I then brought down the heavenly light and completed the "As If" ceremony without awakening the alter. The fusing was accomplished without a hitch, and the core was able to describe the events as if he was the one that actually did those things.

I expect to be criticized for not getting the sleeping alter's permission. Since the core was being placed in danger for his life or the lives of others if the alter drove home drunk and caused a serious accident, I decided this was a case of "*duty to warn*" and proceeded on that principle. It is important I am able to think outside the box while always trying to do no harm. I must be willing to take a chance with the core's approval and do something new or different for the good of the client.

Case #4

PROBLEM: Fighting constant death wish

This case is about a woman grieving the death of her mother and facing the possible early demise of her spouse. She is chronically depressed and very negative. Even after the fusion of multiple alters, and overwhelming evidence to the contrary, she still feels guilty that she did not do enough for her mother during the final months of her illness. She has a constant death wish but, fortunately, she's afraid to take her own life.

Earl Flora

Process:

I was getting frustrated. Yes, it takes a lot to frustrate me, but I was sure other alters were at least co-conscious with her and exacerbating her negativity and guilt. I was getting nowhere asking if there were others inside intensifying her death wish. I was assured by the subconscious mind there was no one else but the core.

Suddenly, I realized what I thought was the real subconscious mind, which does not take over conscious/executive control of the body, was not where the answers were coming from.

So I asked CT, "*Do you ever come out and take control of the body?*"

She answered, "*Yes.*"

With that I said, "*On the count of three, you will be in the conscious mind and the core will step back, but listen to what transpires.*"

I counted one, two, three and the alter giving the wrong information was in the conscious mind. She answered to the birth name, as did the core, so it became apparent I had mistaken her for being the core and missed her being separate. By its innate design, I must never lose sight the system's main mode of operation is hiding.

At times I've had to say, "*No one can block me*" if I encounter resistance. I have found it works like "clockwork" every time. (Note: See exception in "Situations to Avoid" in CHAPTER ELEVEN. Be sure to say, "*No one can block me!*" with conviction and authority.

I digress for a moment to make a point. At the beginning of therapy I insist on an understanding that I will always be honest with them and I expect all of them never to lie to me. What I missed was the fact that when I would ask the core if she was hearing any voices inside, CT was the part answering "*No*" and I thought it was the core. CT was telling me the truth because CT was not hearing any voices.
Back to the subject.

Then They Were One

Upon questioning, it became apparent this alter had an agenda that included harassing the core to the point she would take her own life and go to heaven to be with all her departed relatives. The alter was not sure whether the core would end up in Heaven if she committed suicide, but since the alter did not kill herself she would be there.

What is interesting in this case is most alters do not think they are any part of the core. They do not realize if they get the core to kill herself they will in fact be just as dead. However, this alter knew that.

I faced a dilemma: She was so negative I could not chance joining her at this time for fear she might overwhelm the core and act on the death wish. She felt the core had messed up all her life and did not deserve to live. I offered to send her to any place on earth or, for that matter, anyplace in the universe. (Note: I just realized no alter has ever asked me to send him or her to Heaven.) She chose Disney World. So with the magical count of three, I whisked her off to an all-expenses-paid get-away where she had VIP status so she would not have to wait in line for the rides. With that said, she was gone.

I brought the core back and questioned her at length why she could not see God's blessings in her life. She revealed it was in the persona of the "teacher mother" to experience a positive outlook on life. With that information I invited her to come out and talk with me about the situation. When she appeared she said she was tired and needed to rest, but after a short discussion she agreed to join the core. After the "As If" ceremony, there was a definite change in the countenance of the core: smiling, good eye contact and an air of positive expectation. When she left she expressed an upbeat, *"Have a good weekend."*

Now, I still had more work to do to assure a more positive core before I brought back the negative alter to join her.

Several weeks passed and finally it was agreed that the negative alter should be joined. Her attitude had changed while she was in Disney World. Both parties agreed and the "As If" ceremony was conducted and then they were "ONE".

Over a period of time the strong urge to kill herself dissipated. She continues in therapy working on developing adaptive coping skills. As she makes progress and her ability to cope without switching we will start titrating her sessions. Once she has not dissociated for a period of six months the subconscious would have lost the ability to fully dissociate/create new alters.

She may need further adjustment-type therapy but not for dissociation. However, if for some reason a new alter is brought into being, it is a simple matter to integrate them. As of this writing she has stayed together and decided to end therapy.

Case #5

PROBLEM: Diabetic client, children alters eating sweets

Process:

Once I was able to identify which alters were eating the sweets while the core was not conscious, I offered them the opportunity to have a candy shop and a lunchroom inside if they promised not to eat anything on the outside. Inside, they could eat all they wanted. To prevent them from eating on the outside, I told them if they ate on the outside then all their goodies will automatically disappear inside.

Being children they had to test my words. I learned this in a later session when their blood sugar was way out of control. I asked CT, *"What caused it?* She said, *"The children were eating on the outside because I took all inside food away."* It took me a minute to realize that the suggestion had worked. The moment they ate on the outside the inside sweets and lunchroom vanished instantly.

Then They Were One

I invited the alter to come out and talk with me about the situation. She said, *"You took away the candy!"* I reminded her she had promised not to eat on the outside. I also reminded her of the consequences of losing the inside food and sweets. She confessed she had eaten some of the cookies they were baking for a party. I reminded her that sweets did not hurt her because she was still a little girl, but the grown-up core had developed a serious disease called diabetes and it could cause her to die.

There were three child alters involved. I gave all of them their own soda fountain, candy supply and lunchroom inside where they could eat whatever they wanted but told them they would instantly lose individual privileges if they ate outside. I had to reinforce it several times before they completely stopped eating outside. There would be a problem if the body was eating in a restaurant or at a party and one or more of the children came out to enjoy the occasion. It was agreed, at such occasions, they could come out, but they would not eat while on the outside.

To verify whether there were soda fountains inside, I instructed the core personality to *"Close your eyes and tell me what you see inside."* I was careful not to ask a leading question, so what she saw was what was going on inside her head. She reported, *"They have soda shops inside and were having a good time."* (Note: This also works for smoking cessation, dieting, over-spending and careless driving.)

These types of interventions serve three purposes:
- It prevents lesser alters from innocently harming the body.
- It serves notice on the core personality that she cannot cheat and blame it on another personality.
- It brings three alters together with a shared experience which speeds up the final fusion.

Case #6

PROBLEM: One alter is hurting the core as a way to control and/or punish her

Process:

It has been my experience what appears to be self-abusive, self-mutilation and suicide attempts, for the most part but not always, are the result of a young male alter who has taken the role of a misguided protector, abuser and/or parent. I have seen them as young as five. This particular alter utilizes those techniques perpetrated on the childhood body. This has been his responsibility from a very early age. Usually he is not aware of the passage of time. He may still see her as a little girl not as an older woman.

After we established the core personality was not harming herself, I asked my co-therapist who is causing the cutting, burning and bruising. Once that alter was identified, I sought to bond with him, never critical of his actions. I avoided putting him on the defensive and concentrated on bonding and building rapport. I gave him, as I do to all, unconditional positive regard. I congratulated him on his steadfastness in parenting the system. I asked him what he likes and dislikes about his job.

He told me hurting her was the only way he could get her to do her chores or maintain control over her. A trust was built when I started asking him if he needed any help. I began suggesting how he could accomplish his goals without injuring her. Being compartmentalized himself, he was in a time lock. He had a one-dimensional mind set and that was to get her to do her chores, day in and day out. He was very resistive to change. Change was not part of his time-locked mind. He probably thought I was crazy suggesting he change anything.

Then They Were One

After he rejected every suggestion, I realized drastic measures needed to be implemented if he was going to change. In the beginning he, as most all of the alters, totally rejected the reality that they shared the same body, and with good reason. They had either stayed the same age or aged in direct proportion to the time they had been in the conscious mind.

I asked him to take a look at his bruised legs and explain how the bruises got there. I asked him to explain the cigarette burns on his stomach or the cuts on his arms. Since he didn't feel the pain he didn't have an explanation. Remember, I am dealing with a young child even though he is in an adult's body, so logic had its limitations.

Since reason had already failed at this point, and it's been my experience it never had a chance, it was time for a reality check. I asked him if he caused any of the injuries on his body. Of course, he denied doing it. But the fact is there was only one body and he needed to know the truth. It was time for an object lesson.

So I told him, *"From now on, when you cause pain on anybody you will feel the same pain. You can believe me and stop hurting her or hurt her and feel your pain. It's your choice. One, two, three."*

(Note: Whenever I give this type of instruction I always energize it by counting one, two three. I used it on my sons growing up and I do not remember ever getting to three before they responded. For some reason it has the effect of actualizing the command. I would love to hear an explanation for its acceptance as some sort of seal of authority. I have two thoughts: it could be a derivative of invoking the Trinity when closing a prayer or it might be what is said at the start of a race, as in "on your mark, get set, go.")

He laughed and said, *"That won't work. I do whatever I want."*

By the next session, guess what? He's not into pain! He was mad at me for hurting him. This opened the door to engage in a deeper dialogue.

I said, "*How could I have hurt you when I was nowhere near you?*"

He said, "*I don't know, but when I hurt her, I felt it!*"

I said, "*Well, you wouldn't believe me when I told you that you shared the same body with her. What do you think now?*"

He's still not sure. He said, "*How can that be? I'm male and she's female.*"

I always try to put myself in their shoes. To be honest it wouldn't make any sense to me either, but it's true. I told him, "*It is the truth that sets us free.*" If I'm patient, they come around.

I once again explained, "*Every one of you shares the one body, you at an earlier age and others at different ages. When any of you are in the conscious mind or out, you are at the body's present age and counting.*"

He was facing a dilemma: How could he maintain control of the core personality without hurting himself? One suggestion that works is to encourage them to open up their own dialogue as the therapy progresses. At this point in the therapy, I am actively suggesting the best way to solve this problem is for him to join her. Being together, he will still be the motivator for the body to get the chores done in a timely manner. I explained he has the motivation in his little body, whereas she has the strength in a mature body. As one adult body, they will have both the motivation and the energy to accomplish their combined goals. They eventually fused and it worked exactly as I had predicted. *It's synergism all over again.*

Case #7

PROBLEM: A 7-year-old male protector is blocking therapy

A female teenage alter has been reliving the trauma weekly for 14 years. She is crying out for resolution, and the 7-year-old male protector pops out and demands I stop trying to help her.

Then They Were One

Process:

As many other therapist do, I encourage my clients to keep paper and pen handy and a small spiral notebook so alters are able to write to me in between sessions. It was in just such an occasion that I received the following paraphrased note about abuse suffered at the hands of her boyfriend:

"How long will this go on? How can he beat me every week, on the same day, at the same time, in the same clothes, in the same weather while he's in New York and I'm here? Is this 'déjà vu' or what? I can't stand it. He kicks me in the stomach, bangs my head on the floor and calls me bad names. When will it stop?"

While I was explaining the situation to the core personality, out pops the 7-year-old male protector. In very strong tones he orders me to stop. I explained she was being abused every week for 14 years and I could stop the beatings.

In a callous voice he said, *"She deserved it!"*

Nothing I said changed his mind.

He challenged me saying, *"There's nothing you can do. I will block you!"*

As a last resort, since I was getting nowhere I simply said, *"On the count of three you will be asleep. One, two, three."* With that, I was told he was asleep, and the core personality was back.

After a brief discussion, it was agreed the female teenage alter would be joined. After the "As If" ceremony, the core reported having had spotty memories of her own, about the beatings and other abuses while pregnant with the boyfriend's baby. She instantly acquired the rest of the story and was able to tell me just what happened after the blanks were filled in with the joining of the other alter. She reported feeling no pain that the alter felt before the fusion. The core explained she thought she blacked out during the beatings, but now realized she simply dissociated at those times.

Earl Flora

(Note: It is not my general practice to arbitrarily put alters to sleep, but there are times when it is expedient for the good of the client. It did not harm him. I have never had to hospitalize an alter to effect a positive outcome. It is important to establish authority to meet any misguided challenges from whomever inside. In this case, I feel it was justified as he was heartless and blocking therapeutic progress.)

(Note: Life is a learning process. I do not know why this truth took so long for me to learn. We write about alters being brought into the conscious mind to abreact and give up the negative affect, but miss, at least in my case, *the truth that they are living in a constant state of reliving the trauma as long as they are compartmentalized. It's not like they are unconscious to their personal hell, they live it 24/7.* This definitely throws a different light on the urgency of the situation!)

CHAPTER ELEVEN - SITUATIONS TO AVOID

Case #1, When joining an alter, always join the alter to the core, not the other way around:

REASON:

The alter is usually younger than the core and holds earlier life memories. The core has more life experience than the alter. For whatever reason, the core has always been able to assimilate the new life experience and integrate it into its chronological order along the life line without any difficulty. (Note: It has been my observation that the subconscious mind is responsible for the assimilation not the conscious core.) It is a *marvelous* event to observe. With the integration, it's like witnessing the birth of a brand-new person. With each successive integration, I witness the changes that bringing these two life experiences together have on the conscious mind.

What happens if you put the core into the alter, even if you say you are building the core? (Note: It is essential that the subconscious mind understands exactly what I am saying in going through the "As If" ceremony and then follows the instructions to the letter, to guarantee they cannot separate. Having thus said, I am in the process of developing a pattern of behavior in the subconscious mind that is repeatable and will have the desired outcome, time after time. We know the subconscious mind takes suggestions literally regardless, in most cases, of the outcome. It neither reasons nor corrects our mistakes. It only follows orders exactly as it perceives them to be.)

So here is what happens if you allow yourself, as I was, to be coerced into reversing the process. I asked the core to look inside to see if anyone wanted to join. The core said there was a young girl that wanted to join. As in most cases, I invited the alter into the consciousness. After determining that indeed, this very young alter wanted to join, I tried to get her to just step back and let the core come into full consciousness.

Whether she did not understand or was obstinate, she pouted and refused to follow my instructions. So, I figured I could complete the fusion with her in the consciousness, as long as I emphasized that in the joining she would be entering the core and not the other way around.

However, when the "As If" ceremony was over the core reported feeling very, very heavy and her mind was completely blank. It did not take long for me to realize the core had actually been fused into the young girl's, limited life experience mind. It was analogous to putting the cart before the horse. It overloaded the system.

I believe the subconscious mind (CT) followed my instructions explicitly, as far as the mechanism went. Even though I clearly said, *"As we continue to form the core we know as (name omitted),"* CT put the greater life force not in the conscious mind into the lesser life force in the conscious mind. That is tantamount to overloading an electrical circuit and blowing the circuit breaker.

SOLUTION:

So what to do? I quickly reversed the "As If" ceremony. I said, *"On the count of three, the ceremony that joined these two will now be reversed and they will come apart. One, two, three."* and separated them. Then I asked the core how she felt. She reported having her sensorium back, so I had her stay in the conscious mind and had the little girl brought to her on the inside and affected the fusion in the normal way. When she opened her eyes this time, it was the normal reaction with no loss of cognition. She reported acquiring the life experience held by the young girl.

Case #2, Avoid power struggles:

REASON:

Besides the obvious, he/she has been the one who has protected the system over its life time by various techniques, including scaring people away by presenting as demons, devils or just plain oppositional behavior. You name it and they have probably used it successfully.

By challenging them, you are empowering them. They see you as the enemy that needs to be driven off for the protection of the system (e.g., mainly the children). They have a job to do and you are interfering — period!

SOLUTION:

So what to do? To the best of my recollection I have encountered only one situation where force did not succeed. It was a case of a middle-aged lady who was in therapy over a period of years, under the care of several mental health and medical personnel, with little or no success. She had been in my care for about a year, experiencing the weirdest of symptoms her psychiatrist, medical doctor and I had ever seen, mostly physical, when faced with difficult decisions.

In the initial intake she had denied hearing voices or any other DID systems. However, as it often happens, during the therapy process one alter or the other spontaneously became conscious and the "cat was out of the bag." (Note: My style of writing is not always clinical due to my wide range of life experiences before I became a psychologist. So please grant me that. I mean no disrespect to my more academic readers.)

Earl Flora

To continue: Once I started identifying various alters, out pops her protector in all his rage demanding that I stop interfering with them. The resistance was based on an early life trauma that was covered up to keep the family from being killed by the perpetrator. In spite of the fact the perpetrator was no longer alive, the protector had her in a panic, even before they came into my office. As a result, no meaningful therapy could be accomplished.

To cut to the chase, all attempts to reason with the protector failed. He would not respond to my trying to put him to sleep, move him back or send him to a distant location of his choice. He steadfastly stood in the way. So I decided to put a barrier around him so he could not interfere. That worked for a couple of sessions and progress was made. Then he figured out how to get around the barrier, so I put a ceiling over the barrier so that he was unable to get out. This had the effect of further enraging him. He tried to widen a crack in the concrete walls so the alters could hear him threaten them if they cooperated with me. He kept them in hysterics.

I tried everything I had successfully used in numerous sessions with others, but since she was hysterical when she was in my office, based on a reasonable degree of psychological certainty, I told the family, further therapy was contraindicated until she could control her emotions.

I'm sorry to report, as of this date, she neither has been back to my office nor requested her files.

(Note: In hindsight, this could have been my one case that could have benefited from being hospitalized. On the other hand, she was under the care of a psychiatrist and was on antianxiety medication all the time to no avail.)

CHAPTER TWELVE - VALIDATION

PROBLEMS:

1. The fear of *iatrogenesis*, a Greek word meaning *"brought on by the healer,"* has been associated with DID/MPD. Flora (1988) found there are critics that insist a naïve therapist created altered states of consciousness using hypnosis on hysterical clients who were motivated by secondary gain and then simply erased them via hypnosis. (Thigpen and Cleckley, 1984)

2. Therapists also have been accused of creating "False Memories."

3. How can one be certain that the alters are not simply a figment of the client's imagination or the creation of the therapist?

ANSWERS:

To the first criticism: Iatrogenesis

I never induce a formal trance in a suspected DID client. I simply engage them in a dialogue as I would anybody. Nothing suggestive of entering any trance state is ever mentioned. But that does not overcome the criticism. It has been my experience they are in a constant state of self-hypnosis. As such, they are highly suggestible which allows the "As If" fusion ceremony to accomplish its purpose.

To guard against accidentally creating an interject, I rarely use leading questions. I hesitate to give an example of this as there are so many variations on this theme. However, one example would be to simply instruct the core, *"Close your eyes and tell me what you see."* Omit including *"inside your mind"* or *"how many alters you see."*

Finally, the therapist cannot rewrite the actual personal history verified by the completion of the "External Dissociative Identity Check List Observed by Others" found in the APPENDIX.

To the second criticism: False memories

There are many incidences where creating false memories are in the best interest of the client. However, they are all directed toward the future, not the past. I have purposely created false memories when I send a malevolent alter, with her approval, to Disneyland for a week to keep him/her from inflicting pain, suffering and/or death on the whole system. On more than one occasion I have put alters/interjects to sleep to protect the system. In one case I sealed the persecutor (who may be an interject) in a maximum-security cell to keep him from getting the core to kill herself.

At other times I have created a fancy bedroom to calm down an alter and keep her occupied inside. On more than one occasion I have created an internal candy shop for the child alters, who repeatedly come out at night and devoured all the sweets in the house. All the while, the core cannot figure out why she's gaining weight, even though she is on a diet.

To keep the core from being fired for incompetence, I created an internal "play office" to keep young alters from coming out at work. (Note: I have many of these examples, but for the sake of space, these will suffice for now. They are limited only by my imagination.)

This example is not exactly a false memory, rather the implication of "*the truth to effect a positive outcome.*" As mentioned before, there are times when I have told protectors who were using physical pain to control the core, "*From now on, whenever you inflict pain on anybody else you will feel the same pain, on the count of three.*" This has been very successful in breaking down the sense of separateness experienced by almost, if not all, alters before they have been identified.

To the third criticism: Figment of imagination

Working with older adults is difficult, if not impossible, to acquire firsthand corroboration as to the validity of the life experiences that, in effect, caused the compartmentalization in the first place. However, this is not necessary to effect final fusion.

But working with children and teenagers, it has been possible to receive corroboration, from the parent, as to the validity of the trauma that led to the dissociation.

In the case of a 17-year-old male, his mother was able to tie the alters' birth ages with specific traumatizing life events, (e.g., being in an incubator after birth, falling out of the crib when he was 1 and his parents divorcing when he was 6 years old.) In a very bazaar description, the core could not describe what the 5-year-old boy was wearing because his clothes kept changing right before his eyes. In other words, they were in constant motion. First one style and/or color shirt or pants were described and then something quite different was visualized next. It all happened so rapidly that the scene was not long enough for him to fully describe the clothes. We were both baffled by this strange phenomenon. I, for one, had no explanation until his mother joined us at the end of his session.

After she heard the description of her son's "bowl-shaped haircut," she said he was 5 to 6 years old at that time. Without knowing the difficulty he encountered in trying to describe the boy's clothes, she said, *"He would keep changing his clothes! He would come down dressed for school and go right back up and change into something different almost constantly, until I would stop him."*

Finally, as stated above, the therapist cannot rewrite the actual history verified by the completion of the "EXTERNAL DISSOCIATIVE IDENTITY CHECK LIST OBSERVED BY OTHERS" or the "CHILD DISSOCIATIVE CHECK LIST" *found* in the APPENDIX.

By my definition, any apparent alter states of consciousness created by outsiders and/or the client's imagination are simply interjects and simply disintegrate in some fashion or another when involved in the "As If" fusion ceremony.

Finally the therapist's responsibility is to discover and identify authentic altered states of consciousness and then resolve their hurt, pain and suffering, thus fusing them with the core personality. In fact, they are the only ones that can be fused with the core personality and take their proper place on the "time line" of life.

CHAPTER THIRTEEN - STRANGE SITUATIONS

First example: A 60-year-old female started her period

A 60-year-old divorced female began her session by reporting feeling heavyhearted and tired. In the course of the session, she reported something very strange happening to her since we last met, namely that she had started her period. She was sure it was not simply a vaginal discharge.

Procedure

Thinking the situation was the result of a much younger alter who was co-conscious, I asked her to close her eyes and asked CT to "*Bring the alter that was responsible for the 'period' forward so she could be seen.*" Immediately the core described a rather obese 17-year-old high school student that wanted a man and worried a lot because she cannot get a date. CT identified her as (name omitted).

After I joined them, the core was able to describe, in detail, why she was having a period. She said, "(Name omitted) *had trouble with her period. It was very thick and heavy.*"

I always ask for a sort of debriefing and/or a description of any change in their perception after the fusion. She said, "*Now the room seems lighter than when I came in. I don't feel so weighted.*"

In the next session, she reported her period had stopped.

Second example: White light felt like mint toothpaste, alter squeezes into the core

During the above "As If" ceremony, the core described the pure white light that came down from Heaven above as feeling like "*mint toothpaste*" and the alter sort of squeezing into her as the "As If" ceremony proceeded. (Note: I have no idea what that was all about, but the important thing is they are together and her period stopped.)

Not to get bogged down in the details, but I'd like to point out it is the subconscious mind interpreting my instructions. I, as the orchestra leader, am only the conductor. The rest of their mind is made up of musicians (metaphorically speaking) who are interpreting my instructions. I do not know if other parts of the mind are interfering at times, but I keep focused on the outcome and do not second guess the process.

I'm pragmatic. If it gets the desired results, that's great! And yes, I'm all for expanding the process, as I trust some of my readers will take this and run with it to new and better methods of resolving their separateness.

Third example: Being kept off balance by a man standing in a rocking boat

During the same session as above, the woman reported feeling off balance. I said, *"Close your eyes and see the alter that is causing you to feel off balance."*

She said, *"The guy in the boat is keeping me off balance. It's my dad!"*

Procedure: I directed the boat to come to the shore and had her father get out of the boat and proceed up to her. As soon as he was close enough. I instructed them to take each other's hands and continued with the "As If" ceremony. As soon as she opened her eyes she said, *"That one was sucked up and gone. They said I didn't need any more of that. Sucked up and gone like breaking through cellophane. And they took all of it. None of that's useful. Now my vision is crystal clear. I feel a lot better."* (Note: She attributed the "They" to be the Triune God.) I consider the father to have been an "interject.

I know this is redundant, but I feel it is important, especially to the novice, to fully comprehend the difference between a true alter and an interject. I have read elsewhere about therapists describing how they agreed for certain alters to die. Well, I think you would have to use electric shock therapy to eradicate a true life event or suffer some type of stroke or brain infection to kill a true life event. In my experience, interjects are figments of the system's imagination or some outside person's imagination being suggested to the system. As such, they assume the form of a true alter, but lack the substance of a true alter, (e.g., "in vivo" compartmentalized via trauma. As such, in the integration process, they simple vanish. (Note: See interjects in CHAPTER FOUR under "DEFINITIONS.")

Fourth example: Satan, as a four-legged impish rat-goat with a beard like a goat, horns and a tail

(The following is a direct quote made by a middle-aged widow in my clinical notes.)

"I've come from being afraid of the ladies at church to feeling comfortable around them. (However, while) listening to two ladies talking about spiritual warfare having to combat demons, I got so ill I had to leave. My stomach turned and I had this memory. She (adopted mother) would curse me in many ways. It hasn't left yet. Help me find it?" (Note: "It" was referring to why she became sick and had to run out of the church.)

(Note: The incident took place two days earlier.)

Procedure

I said, *"Close your eyes. Now the ONE making you sick will come to you. What do you see?"*

She covered her eyes with both hands. Her face flushed and she suddenly clasped her hand in her lap in silence.

I asked, *"Are you going to tell me?*

Earl Flora

She replied, *"No! Do I have to?"*

I said, *"Only if you want me to help you."*

She reluctantly continued. *"It's a four-legged impish rat-goat with a beard like a goat. It stands (upright) on its two (hind) legs. It has horns (and) a long tail with hair at the end."*

I said to my CT, *"Tell her what this character is."*

The core answered, *"Satan."*

I asked, *"How long has it been there?"*

The core answered, *"All my life!"*

I asked, *"What is its purpose?"*

The core answered, *"To make me miserable."*

I asked, *"Did the mother put it in you?"*

The core answered, *"She always said I was Satan's child."*

I continued, *"The fact is, you are a child of God."*

The core answered, *"I can't accept that."*

I said, *"The Satan figure is a myth. I invoke the love of God, demonstrated on the cross, to fill you completely, overshadowing the beast, causing it to incinerate, dissolve as a vapor. Going up into the atmosphere, into outer space never to return."*

With that the core said, *"It's gone. It just wasn't there."*

Whether it was just a figment of her imagination or real, it was with her for the most part of her life and now it was gone.

I asked CT, *"Is it gone?"*

Then They Were One

She acknowledged that it was gone, but there were others.

I asked, "*How many?*"

CT said, "*A lot.*"

The core spoke up and said, "*I was (am) demon possessed.*"

To keep her from panicking, I said, "*Close your eyes, without seeing demons or interjects. I will spell the sentence 'You are demon possessed.'* I spelled it backwards "**s d r a w k c a b d e s s e s s o p n o m e d e r a u o Y** *to erase the suggestion that brought them into the mind in the first place, as if they were never there, on the count of three. One, two, three.*"

The core said, "*They just disappeared.*"

I asked CT, "*Did we get them all?*"

The core said, "*I feel better. I believe it kept me from going forward. I traveled long and hard to get to this point and I couldn't break the power.*"

(NOTE: I do not believe these were real demons. I believe they were interjects created when the adopted mother accused her of being a child of Satan over and over again.)

To eliminate interjects, in addition to "inadvertently" (thinking they were true alters) trying to fuse them, I simply reverse the process in which they were created. I do not need to know how they got there, all I say is, "*On the count of three the process which created you will be reversed and you will be gone,* one, two, three."

Researching attitudes from her birth country revealed "half-breed" babies were referred to as "Tuigi," (translated "child of a foreign devil.")

Realizing the severe prejudice in her native country, is it plausible that as an infant this word was spoken in her presence over and over again? If so, then the demon interjects were well entrenched in her mind probably from birth. You can almost hear the attending midwife or whoever was there for the delivery saying, "She's a Tuigi."

Fifth example: Mother-in-law with her hands tightly wrapped around my clients neck

A different middle-aged female called, very upset because the voices had come back. She requested an unscheduled appointment ASAP. As it was, I had a cancellation for early afternoon, so I asked her to come in then.

(Note: She was so upset because during the last session she stated she had not heard any thoughts out loud since the last integration.)

Procedure

At the beginning of the session, after she reported hearing a voice in her head, I explained to her that just because she was not hearing her thoughts out loud (since the last fusion) was not a guarantee there were no other alters. I reminded her that throughout her therapy sessions, alters are internally observing the integration process, as part of her primary defense mechanism. Being very intelligent, they can alter their behavior to avoid detection. However, eventually they will have to expose themselves.

(Note: So as a therapist, I need to be careful not to jump to the conclusion that full integration has occurred simply because they are not hearing internal voices anymore. See section on length of therapy in CHAPTER FIFTEEN.)

Then They Were One

The following is her account: "*I woke up this morning, got ready and went to work. When I arrived at work, I discovered I was not scheduled today. I went back home and went back to bed. I was awakened by a voice inside my head shouting, 'Get up and go to work! Get up! You gotta go to work!' I was bordering on panic.*"

With that, I instructed her, "*Close your eyes and you will see the person who was shouting at you.*"

With eyes closed, she turned to her the right and said, "*It's a rather large woman, like my mother-in-law. She didn't like me. She caused me so much anxiety. When I was pregnant she insisted I set the table and eat even though I was so sick. I got up and left the table. The whole thing was to make me sicker.*"

I instructed her, "*Take the lady's hands in yours.*"

Suddenly, with her eyes still closed, she grabbed her throat by both hands, in a choking fashion. With that, I accelerated the "As If" ceremony to effect the fusion as quickly as possible!

After the light went up she opened her eyes and said, "*When the white light came down it wouldn't let her come near me, I heard, 'Let go of her hands. We can take her.' (With that) she turned to dust. When the white light went up it sucked all the dust up like a vacuum cleaner.*"

To my surprise, she still had her hands wrapped around her throat, so I instructed her, "*Take your hands and use them to pull her hands away from your throat.*"

With that, her hands came away from her throat and she said, "*It was the lady's hands around my throat.*"

This is another case where I was unknowingly dealing with an "interject." The beautiful part of that is the system somehow overcomes my ineptitude. Thank goodness!

The lesson to be learned again is I do not have all the answers. I'm thinking one thing is happening when in fact something entirely different is transpiring. From the beginning, I emphasize that I am only the facilitator, whereas it is a collaborative process working with the subconscious mind and my internal co-therapist that effects the change. I am always grateful when their system countermands my instructions when they do not exactly fit the situation. This speaks well for their superior intelligence. (Note: I stand in awe at the power of one's mind.)

She said, *"I feel clearer and a lot more positive."*

Sixth example: The reluctant Virgin Mary and three others

Procedure

The core said, *"We still need to deal with the Virgin Mary and those in the front yard of my house. They are a female and two males. One of the males comes out when I'm experiencing high anxiety and basically tells off whoever was causing it."*

With the core's permission, I invited the Virgin Mary out and engaged her in a dialogue. I assured her she was a valuable part of the life. By joining the core, she would be in the conscious mind for as long as the core was in the conscious mind. She would be in a better position to effect the kind of outcomes she was now only able to suggest.

After we joined the Virgin Mary, the core described her as, *"Petite, with a halo and wearing a golden robe. She was the all-loving mother, no matter what. Anything that separated us was severed when the light came down. It was like Velcro between us. Then we were one. Now I'm back in my first grade classroom. Maybe that's when it happened."*

I asked, *"Compared to when you came in today, how do you feel now?"*

Then They Were One

She said, *"I don't feel 'floaty,' anxious or confused."*

Suddenly the core said: *"The lady in the front yard said, 'The fuck you are! We are very happy here.'"*

There was no time to address this declaration, since it happened at the end of the session. As it turned out, after observing the Virgin Mary joining, the two men and one woman made it very clear they were very happy being in the front yard and were not in the least interested in joining. (Note: Prior efforts to get them to join had failed.).

The core called that night upset, and requested a session the next day before she went to work. She was afraid the male would come out, tell customers off and jeopardize her job. At first, as before, they refused to join. I invited the main man out and engaged him in an evaluation of his technique. He demonstrated how his telling everybody off was creating more problems than it solved because of his limited life experience. I explained how the system needed to possess his ability to set boundaries and stand up for themselves if they were to survive. After I explained, as a part of the whole, his attributes, coupled with a lifetime of acquired wisdom, would be invaluable in the decision-making process, he agreed to join. After he joined, it did not take much persuasion to get the other two to join during the same session.

A few sessions later her manager commented on what a change had occurred in her performance from just a few months ago when he was ready to fire her. Now she is so personable, positive and highly productive, compared to how she was before (she started therapy). "That's high praise/progress!" (Mine)

Seventh example: A guy with a sword

Procedure:

This was someone the core had identified earlier.

She said, *"A voice in my right ear said, 'Let's join the guy with the sword.'"*

I said, "*Close your eyes and see him.*"

She said, "*I see a guy with a sword. He's as big as the room. He's crystal blue with the sword of truth. He's gyrating with his arms outstretched above his head.*"

I did not engage the "guy with the sword" in conversation. Rather I instructed her to take his hands and finished the "As If" ceremony without further comment.

I had not mentioned it before, but from the beginning, when I asked her to take the alter's hands and embrace each other, she physically outstretched her arms in front of her, while seated, wrapping her arms around the alter. As they came together, her arms would end up hugging herself. That way, I was able to judge the alter's size. True to form, in this case her arms were outstretched as far as she could, indicating a very large man. As the "As If" ceremony progressed, I observed her arms slowly begin to fold inward, until by the end, her arms were hugging herself. (Note: This was not something I suggested, it was the way she perceived my suggestion. She is one of a few who physically out stretches their arms.)

After the light went up she said, "*I had a bit of a headache on my right side, but now it's gone away. Right now I feel centered.*"

Eighth example: Compromise, a trip to Disneyland

I ran into a road block while making progress joining alters in a middle-aged female when she decided to have corrective surgery. There was a complete shutdown of willing alters to join. It took a little detective work to discover the reason for the shutdown. The remaining alters had acquired insight into just how the integration process worked. If they joined they would no longer be separate where they could exercise independent control of the body.
The part they objected to was sharing consciousness during surgery and painful post op.

Procedure

I negotiated a compromise. (Note: Remember even though many of the alters are children, I always treat them with respect and as much as possible wait for their agreement before proceeding.) Having thus said, I suggested if they would agree to join after all the surgery was completed and she had recuperated, I would send all of them to Disneyland, set them up in the best hotel, allow them to have all the room service they wanted, be accorded first in line privileges and enjoy themselves at my expense until they see her back in therapy after the surgery is over. (Note: This is another example where creating a false memory was therapeutically indicated.)

They agreed and I simply said, *"On the count of three all of you will be in Disneyland, one, two, three."* Just to make sure they were there, I asked the core to close her eyes and tell me what she saw.

She closed her eyes and said, *"I see them walking down Main Street."*

(Note: As of this date she has not returned to therapy. All attempts to contact her have failed.)

Ninth example: A basketful of babies

A longtime client who dropped out of therapy several years earlier had returned following the loss of a loved one. Rapport was quickly reestablished and we made rapid success joining alters. It appeared we were very close to complete success.

The following is why I give six more months after final fusion without voices and/or dissociation to be sure there are no fragments lurking in the recesses of the mind. We had supposed she was complete, but in this session she reported seeing a basketful of babies since her last session.

It made no sense to her. But knowing the story of her earlier life I connected it with her being left on the doorsteps of a foreign country's orphanage, soon after her birth.

I asked her to close her eyes and see the basket, which she did. She counted five babies from 6 months to 18 months of age. At this point she hadn't made the connection. I explained the five babies probably represented five alters who had survived five different traumas. As such they appeared as five different babies, when in fact they were all her, compartmentalized. With that explanation, she began to sob and covered her face with her hands.

It was a very emotional moment of discovery: She said, *"What I was told by my adopted parents was true after all!"*

Procedure:

Continuing to process the feeling of total abandonment, she was reluctant to even approach the basket. It took several tries before she could bring herself to even touch the basket. Finally she garnered enough courage to embrace the basketful of her very early life experiences and allow the "As If" ceremony to be performed.

I instructed her, *"Reach out and embrace all five babies, all at once in your arms at one time."* Then I continued the "As If" ceremony and they were ONE.

These baby alters were the most difficult ones for her to accept. Who wants to know you were branded "the child of the devil" and abandoned by your birth mother? Talk about an attack on one's self-esteem! In that country, as mentioned earlier during the conflict, mixed-breed babies were called "Tuigi."

Tenth example: Living in poverty?

This is about a middle-aged female who has been in therapy for about one year. Some of the context has been altered to protect her identity.

Procedure:

She said, *"I cannot shake the feeling I'm destined to always live in poverty. I've been grumpy and irritable since last session."*

(Note: She had experienced a big disappointment and some interpersonal problems which resulted in the above reaction.)

I said, "*Close your eyes and see if there is a persona that can explain why you felt that way.*"

She said, "*It's Poor Pitiful Pearl*" (Note: A poverty doll she had adopted at age six).

She said, "*I fell in love with that doll.*" (Note: It was apparent the doll had taken on human form in her mind.)

After further discussion, it was agreed that I would join them.

After the "As If" ceremony she said, "*It was a child that joined me. Then I saw the cutest little cottage. Now I have a headache in my eyes. Sounds like it took something out of my head.*" (Note: Apparently she received something that wasn't supposed to be in her head in the first place. See below. It turned out to be the dog in her eye.) "*I saw my aunt. I would go and visit her. She was poor, but kept a spotless house. She gave me a little dog (named) Sue. I loved that dog like it was life itself.*

"*When you did that,* (Referring to what I thought was joining the little girl) *that China doll was right here inside my face and the Poor Pitiful Pearl Doll was on my left side. When she (China Doll) left, the dog shot out of my eyes. Oh my God! I connected the dog with my aunt's poverty. That's where I got my love of poverty. She married poor and everybody in the family took care of her. The dog and the doll were connected to the poverty of my aunt. Everything was neat and clean. She was refined. I'm stunned!*

"*I watch this stuff and still don't believe it, but it makes so much sense. I wonder if I will hold onto the poverty.*"

Upon reflection she said, "*My tears are not for sadness; it's over! All the pieces (alters) want to come in because it's working. I'm not irritate now at all. If I had a metaphor for it, I feel like you put the (phonograph) needle back in the groove.*"

Several sessions later after we had joined what appeared to be the last of the alters, she said, *"For the first time in my life I know who I am."*

Eleventh example: Libido

While I was working with a middle-aged female, joining the few remaining alters, we joined one that held what turned out to be only part of her libido. She reported having difficulty coping with constantly being aroused. Nothing she tried gave her relief. She even went to her physician and received an antidepressant which has, as one of its side effects, the ability to reduce one's sex drive. This did nothing to relieve her problem. We discussed the fact she would need time to adjust to having a libido like the rest of the normal population, but since it was a relatively new sensation she felt overwhelmed.

Procedure: Or, should I say, partial solution in her case.

I had suggested, in several previous sessions, that maybe she still had alters that shared the libido. She insisted she could not find anyone inside as we had joined all of the alters. Well, as in all cases, if a problem is prominent and there are no rational explanations for it, I look inside to see if there is an alter that is co-conscious at times and superimposing her/his problem on the core.

I asked her, *"Close your eyes* (Note: Just a reminder, I seldom perform a formal induction because DIDs are perpetually in a state of self-hypnosis.) *and on the count of the magical three you will see whoever it is that is causing you to feel over-sexed, one, two, three. What do you see?"*

She said, *"There is a very young girl sitting in the corner of the living room, constantly masturbating."*
(Note: Without sounding insensitive, that would keep anybody in a constant state of sexual arousal since that's what it's designed to do.)

Without further delay, I said, *"On the count of three the little girl will be right next to you. One, two, three."*
She said, *"She's next to me."*

I said, *"Take her hands and embrace."* Then I completed the "As If" ceremony and they were one.

I asked, *"Do you notice any change?"*

She said, "There's *"a slight reduction, but not much."*

Several sessions later she said, *"It is still difficult for me to deal with."*

(Note: A review of various DID forum websites revealed this is a very common problem for many DID females. I tried to normalize it with her. I explained this is a problem for the human race in general. It was the discovery of suddenly coming into full-blown libido that was so overwhelming and unsettling to her.

I referred her to her female gynecologist hoping she might be able to offer female advice and/or medication to help her adjust to being a normal female for the first time in her life. The libido, by nature, is highly emotionally charged and in most DID cases will be compartmentalized for the survival of the system.

(Follow-up: After visiting her doctor, it was discovered that in addition to joining her libido alters for the first time, she was premenopausal. Appropriate hormones were prescribed which helped moderate her libido.)

Several sessions later she reported when the medications ran out her libido once again became overbearing. She pleaded with me to see if I could do something to help her not feel so sexually aroused all the time. Since this was an ongoing dilemma, I had given it a lot of thought prior to this session. Since she was no longer actively dissociating, meaning there were no more alters to join, I reasoned, if she wished I would consult her subconscious mind to make sure there were no new alters and ask for permission to create a new altered state of consciousness in which to deposit the libido.

Earl Flora

Without a formal trance, I simply asked her subconscious mind (SM) if it would be permissible for me to create a new altered state of consciousness to contain her libido. SM responded with an "ideomotor" thumbs up (positive) response. With that I said, *"On the count of three the libido will be compartmentalized from the core personality, one, two, three."* SM raised the thumb again, indicating the libido was compartmentalized.

My client verified her libido was gone.

(Note: A word of caution, this was only done at the urgent request of my client! I will be alert to any negative consequences which result from this compartmentalization in the future. She promised to call me ASAP if she has any negative reaction to the compartmentalization.)

If this creates additional problems, we will deal with them after discussing the alternatives and reaching a mutual solution.

This is not a done deal by any means. I will be working with her to find a way to integrate her libido incrementally to give her time to adjust to it. In addition, as this process progresses, I will refer her to a female therapist to help her adjust further.

Continuing with the follow-up: Several sessions later she complained again, that her libido had returned and was driving her crazy 24/7. To cut to the chase, it was decided to induce a formal trance and install a "libido rheostat" in her subconscious mind.
It worked perfectly. She was able to increase her libido and to reduce it from a high of seven to a zero. Even at zero, she reported still feeling mildly aroused. I initiated a post hypnotic suggestion that with certain hand configurations she would automatically see the rheostat in her mind and could adjust it at will. She tried it and reported success.

Then They Were One

Twelfth example: A psychiatrist

A mature female client, working in retail related, "*A customer was complimenting me on how understanding I was. She said I should be a therapist. Suddenly, a male voice came out of my mouth in a commanding tone and said to the customer, 'You are supposed to suffer!' I was so shocked. I excused myself and went into the ladies restroom. I looked in the mirror and I looked crazy and I had a headache.*"

Procedure:

Again without inducing a formal trance, I said, "*Close your eyes and turn your head to the right and you will see him. There he is, one, two, three.*" (Note: In this incidence, since it was clearly a male's voice, I said she would see him.)

I continued, "*Tell me who you see.*"

(Note: There is no advantage to having her turn her head to either the right or the left. But since she is sitting directly across the room in front of me, by turning her head to the right, her head is facing me and I am able to observe her facial expressions.)

She said, "*He's very tall. He's saying, 'You are damaged merchandise.'*"

(Note: To have this make sense, as you will see later, he thinks he's a psychiatrist. Inside her mind, he lives in a psychiatric hospital and is very authoritarian.)

I invited him to come out but he couldn't or wouldn't come out. Upon reflection, I decided to put her in a "deep formal trance" in an effort to try and get him to talk with me. (This is the sort of situation where I will use a formal induction to garner information but not to diagnose DID or to fuse alters.)

Finally he said, *"All this is bullshit with her. She doesn't have a degree!"* (Note: I believe in his first sentence he was referring to the customer. In the second sentence, he is referring to the core.)

In order to acquire background on Sigmund I asked, *"CT, can you tell me about him?"*

CT said, *"He pretends he has a degree."*

I said, *"How old is he?"*

CT said, *"22."*

I asked, *"How old was he when he was created?"*

CT said, *"22."*

(Note: This is a situation where I will bypass the core and speak directly to my CT who is herself an altered state of consciousness. This way I can obtain information unattainable with the core being conscious.)

By this time, my client was fully conscious. She was able to provide relevant history leading up to Sigmund's creation. Again, it was surrounded by a traumatizing event.

To safeguard her identity, I am changing the event to the sudden death of her beloved sister-in-law in a house fire. Coincidentally, her sister-in-law's father was a psychiatrist. All of this coincides with her sister-in-law's funeral date.

To summarize, it was at the funeral service that CT reported the psychiatrist was brought inside the mind to help her cope with the sister-in-law's death and her failing marriage.

I am always interested in how or where the alters/interjects acquired their names. I asked my client if she knew anybody named Sigmund. She told me Sigmund was the name of the street they played on while growing up.

Then They Were One

(Note: Whenever true alters were fused the core acquires their total life experience, along with skills and talents, sometimes instantly, sometimes in dreams and sometimes over a short period of time in the conscious mind.)

Knowing the above, she became frightened with the suggestion that Sigmund was not a true alter but an interject, or figment of her imagination. She was worried she would lose his ability as a psychiatrist.

To be honest, at that point, I did not know what would be the final result. What was clear was that he was a disrupting a factor in her life as long as he remained separate. In these cases, all I can do is draw on my clinical knowledge, attempt to do no harm and move ahead cautiously. So after some discussion with the core as to the options, we agreed to attempt the fusion and deal with the consequences.

All I can say is, "*I'm seldom bored working with this population and in this case the results were anything but boring. On the contrary, they were surprising! I went through the normal 'As If' ceremony, bringing them together to hold hands, embrace, while I brought the light down, etc. After the light went up, I asked her what happened.*"

She said, "*The light came down and he was on the other side of the shaft of light. He didn't disappear. He turned to ridged wood and smelled of burning wood.*"
I said, "*Close your eyes. I will count to three and when I get to three, the process that brought him into existence, in the mind, will be reversed and he will be completely erased, one, two, three.*"

She opened her eyes and said, "*He's gone.*"

She continued, "*Now I remember good experiences of smelling turpentine and paint.*" She recounted how at age 15 she was suicidal. Her teacher took her to a counselor who told her, "*Suicide is selfish. After you are gone, no one will miss you. It's just an act of revenge.*"

She went home and told her mother, "*I feel like I'm coming apart.*" She was taken to a psychiatrist who told her she was suffering from epilepsy, but all the tests were negative. (Note: Another missed diagnosis.)

I said, "*Let's see if the 15 year old is separate. Close your eyes and look around and tell me what you see.*"

She said, "*It's a wide shadow. It's wide behind the wall, sad and lonely.*" She heard a voice saying, "*You're not wanted; you'll never fit in.*"

I said, "*Walk over to the shadow. Now go around in front of the shadow and you will see who is casting the shadow.*"

She said, "*It's a young girl.*"

Tears started flowing down her cheeks and she said, "*This is Easter!*"

I instructed her, "*Reach out, in a jester of love and acceptance to this young girl. Take her in your arms.*" I performed the "As If" ceremony and they were ONE.

Her comments after the fusion were, "*I'm not feeling lonely anymore. I don't feel disconnected. This is a little weird for me. Remember I used to say, 'I didn't connect.'*"

(Note: How appalling that, for over 40 years, this young girl suffered in a compartmentalized world, feeling unloved and unwanted up until now. When in less than a moment, in the twinkling of an eye, all that changed! Now she was loved!)

Thirteenth example: An aborted fetus

Approaching the joining of the final alter, I ask my co-therapist to look inside and tell me what she sees. She reported seeing a very small baby sleeping all by itself. It turned out to be the fetus my client had admitted aborting in her late teens. She had previously reported feeling sad as she reflected on how old he/she would be if she had not had the abortion. (Note: This was not an issue to be processed at this point. That remains for a later session and/or sessions.)

Procedure:

Speaking to the core I said, *"If this is truly an alter it must be joined with you."*

She agreed and I continued, "Close your eyes and look to *your right. See the infant?"*

She said, *"Yes."*

I said, *"Go over and pick up the infant and hold it in your arms."* (Note: I asked if she wanted to know the sex of the infant and she said, *"No."* Since she said no, I had to refer to the infant as '*it*." I continued to administer the "As If" ceremony and joined the infant with her.

With tears in her eyes, she said, *"It came into me and is gone."*

Fourteenth example: Panicking while seated on the floor of a truck

A female client at the clean-up stage of her therapy reported experiencing a panic attack while seated on the floor of a truck she and two friends were using to move furniture. There was only room for two people to sit on the seat, so she volunteered to sit on the floor. She reported panicking after she looked up and saw the trees passing by. She had to force her way up and onto the passenger's lap to stop panicking.

Earl Flora

Procedure:

Once again without any formal induction, I simply said, *"Close your eyes and look inside. On the count of three you will see who was causing you to panic, one, two, three. Tell me what you see."*

She said, *"I see a little girl sitting on the floor board in the back seat of the car in between the other kid's feet. She's looking up and is very scared."*

(Note: this was obviously her at a young age. She was the mixed-race orphan adopted by this abusive family.)

I said, *"Go over to her and I will have her stand up and you can take her by her hands and we will join her with you."*

She said, *"She is afraid to stand up. She's forbidden to stand up and will be kicked by the kids if she tries."*

I said, *"OK. Go over to her and take her by her hands and on the count of three she will let you lift her up to you, one, two, three. Lift her up. Do you have her?"*

She said, *"Yes."*

I said, *"OK. Embrace her."* I performed the "As If" ceremony and they were instantly joined.

Afterward, she was able to elaborate on how the abusive family never let the general public see her when they were driving in the car.

Fifteenth example: Two clinched fists

A female client complaining about her almost-inability to speak in public was asked to close her eyes (Note: No formal induction. She was simply given the instructions and she always responded as if she was under hypnosis.) and see inside who was creating this problem.

At first she reported a shadow-like little girl standing against the cellar wall and being beaten nightly by the adopted father, at the instructions of the adopted mother, after the girl confessed her wrong doings for the day. At this point I noticed both of her hands became clenched fists as she described the abuse with her eyes closed. It was obvious she was moved/upset by the scene she was witnessing.

Procedure:

I asked, "*Describe the person.*"

She said, "*I see a shadow-like figure.*"

I said "*On the count of three you will see the shadow take on the form of the person being abused, one, two, three. What do you see now?*"

She said, "*I see a little girl.*"

After a little reflection, I surmised there must be more than one alter created to take this nightly punishment.

I said, "*If there is more than one alter that takes the punishment let them appear on the count of three, one, two, three. Now tell me what you see.*"
She said, "*There are three girls.*"

It was getting close to the end of the session, so I decided to join only one alter at this time and wait until her next session to join the others since there was so much abuse.

(Note: Keep in mind that during this, her eyes stayed closed as she was witnessing the abuse and both fists remained tightly clenched. To be honest, even though I had never witnessed anything like this before, I did not give it much thought. I was more interested in how the core would handle joining so much abuse history even though I would be joining one out of the three.)

Earl Flora

I instructed her, "*Approach the girl closest to you. Are you there?*"

She said in a very soft voice, "*Yes.*"

I said, "*Take her hands. Do you have them?*"

She said, "*Yes.*"

(Note: I could see, by the expression on her face, she was distressed by touching her.) I speeded up the "As If" fusion ceremony. After I brought the light back up (signaling the end of the "As If" ceremony), it was a few minutes before she opened her eyes.

She looked at her hands clenched into fists and said, "*Why can't I open my hands?*"

It was then I realized, if I were being beaten as she was, I would have clenched fists to deflect the pain and be in an autonomic defensive mode, too.

I said, "*On the count of three, the one with the clenched fists will go to sleep until I see you next week, one, two, three.*"

Nothing happened. She tried to open her fists but could not open either. The fists were still clenched. What was I missing? Well, maybe the suggestion was too general, after all there were two of them.

OK. , I added, "*On the count of three the one who's right hand is clenched into a fist will go to sleep, one, two, three.*" The hand was still clenched.

OK, not to be daunted, I added, "*On the count of three, the one who's right hand is clenched will go into a restful sleep and her hand will automatically relax, one, two, three.*" With a little effort she was able to open and flex her right hand. The left hand was still out of her control.

So, I repeated the above substituting "left hand." Almost immediately she smiled and opened her left hand as well.

Then They Were One

Sixteenth example: Having a headache while being orgasmic

A mature female who had been celibate for many years developed a loving relationship with a very nice gentleman. She complained experiencing a headache while she was having an orgasm. She said, "*It's like I hit a brick wall.*"

Procedure:

I said, "*Close your eyes and on the count of three you will see why you are having headaches during your orgasms, one, two, three.*"

I asked her, "*What do you see?*"

She said, "*It's this large masculine woman standing in Evergreen College, saying, 'We don't need anybody.' At that time I had pushed everybody away from me. Everybody wanted something from me. I said, 'Get away from me.'*"

I asked, "*What is she doing?*"

She said, "*She's just standing there saying, 'We don't need anybody.'*"

I said, "*Walk over to her and take her hands and embrace.*"

She said, "*She's a giant. I can't get my arms around her.*"

With that statement, she extended her arms out in front of her, as wide and as far as she could. As I continued the "As If" ceremony her arms gradually retracted toward her body until she was hugging herself.

Without my asking for feedback, she said, "*I'm hot! She just melted like a candle in the heat. I felt it all the way down to my feet!*"

(Note: Apparently the giant female was causing the headaches by saying "*We don't need anybody*" in order to stop her from having intercourse.)

The human mind never ceases to amaze me with its creativity! As witnessed by the foregoing, it is not necessary to ascertain whether an alter is real or an interject because the subconscious mind will automatically join the alter or remove the interject entirely.

In a later session she reported, *"The quality of my relationship has greatly improved since the headaches went away."*

CHAPTER FOURTEEN - TESTIMONIALS

A Husband's Experience

This testimonial was written by the husband of the very first successful case that has stood the test of time for more than 16 years.

He wrote, "This is dedicated to my loving wife, for without her I wouldn't have had the compassion and strength to see what I had to lose if I was without her in my life. When I was first made aware of what was happening to her, I didn't quite understand it all and really didn't believe what I was being told was happening to her. I knew something wasn't quite right but had no idea as to the cause of her differences in personality and behavior at times. I've known her personally since 1969 when we started dating and now it being 2014 we've been married for 41 years, so I was well aware of her various differences in her behavior prior to being diagnosed with DID. I was quite taken back when I was informed as to what was causing these behavior differences. I didn't know what to think. All I knew is I wanted to do whatever is needed to help her get through this and become the woman and wife that I knew before she started switching to different alters.

When I was allowed to sit in on her sessions with Dr. Flora I was able to see and understand what was going on and how important I was in her overall treatment of her disorder. Throughout the sessions and the months it took for her to overcome and be cured of this disorder I made a commitment to always be open minded and to do my part to not only assist Dr. Flora, but to assist her and be nonjudgmental of anything she does or has to go through.

During the time we were going through the steps to cure her of this behavior disorder it wasn't a bowl of candy. It was more like a can of worms because I never knew what was behind door number two in regards to what might set her off and cause her to dissociate to an alter that could handle the problem at that moment.

Earl Flora

Take for instance this example: We were at the food store and she asked for a certain type of ice cream and without thinking I said, "We didn't need any of that because we already had some ice cream at home." It was right then that an alter, who was known to be at the age of 9, came out and started crying and screamed, "I want my ice cream!"

Well, needless to say she got her ice cream and with that, she came back to the present. It's quite a shock to see this happening, but I was able to get through it all, although it wasn't easy at times. But I did it with Dr. Flora's never-ending guidance and understanding of what she and I were going through.

Since my wife has had all of the alters joined and become a single person within herself for the past number of years, too many to remember, there haven't been any re-occurrences of the alters that were there before. This is quite an accomplishment because, as I know now, stress and various problems within a family can cause a relapse for a person to dissociate again so they can cope with those problems. And there have been quite a few that have come to pass in our lives to cause her to relapse, but thank God she hasn't. I think she has been able to stay together all these past years because she's a very strong person and knows she has someone who will have her back no matter what arises. She knows we can persevere together as a complete unit no matter what gets in our way.

All and all I would not have written this if it wasn't for the fact that I was allowed to sit in on many of my wife's therapy sessions. To obtain the insight and understandings to what was going on was a godsend. Just to be given the smallest amounts of knowledge about all of this and to be told what was going on (e.g., missing time, alter personalities coming out that didn't know who I was) was my life line. I couldn't have made it if it wasn't for Dr. Earl Flora. This man deserves and has my never-ending respect and love."

Note: Used by permission.

Then They Were One

A Successfully Integrated Female

After she heard I was writing a book on DID, she wanted to participate. These are her words transcribed from her handwritten testimony. She wrote extensively concerning the last session about Poor Pitiful Pearl and her lifelong feeling with being poor. (Note: You might want to refer back to the "Poor Pitiful Pearl" session in CHAPTER THIRTEEN, subheading Tenth example: Living in poverty.)

I begin with her writing: "Oh my God! I'd taken on her personal lifestyle! The dog was inside me where my heart is. It grew as I listened to Dr. Flora and then in a dark shadow from the energy it came up my neck and burst out of both eyes gone. I came back as (The core, name withheld).

OK. My first thoughts were, and I said it to Dr. Flora, 'You know it's hard for me to believe any of this stuff because it is so strange. But it makes so much sense' I told him what happened. It felt as if I was centered, feet on the ground. Like the record recorder needle was placed soundly in the groove of the record. It felt right!

Don't think I am so gullible to just follow along and logically say, 'Oh, I understand this process' because I don't! I often am just amazed at the process. But please know my life has changed and it works.

Everyone I know remarks that I am not switching from one personality to another all the time. You see they have been seeing me all the time, but didn't know what they were seeing. I was afraid and nervous all the time because I didn't know who I'd be in any given circumstance. And as years went by, it just got worse. I hit a brick wall when my store manager said, 'Fix it or you are out. I will fire you!' He liked my potential, my ability to get along with anyone I was selling to. I had so much to pick from inside, but I was volatile, unpredictable and, well, odd. I left most people with the impression I was a 'weird' or 'odd' person with a strange take on things.

Earl Flora

It has been hell for me. To want to reach out and have a normal life, but something about me—I could not see it—always ruined it. It is not like that now. The voices, intuitions (false one's), the heartaches, the dread, the confusion, the anger, the craziness, the not being able to perceive a future, the depression—it is all gone now. I don't know why this works but it does.

I have gone from the verge of homelessness and everyone in my life being done with me to getting a 29 percent raise, being named the 'Star Employee,' being liked by some people (and) knowing when I should apologize. I am not afraid all the time. But I am wary of unpredictable personalities (in others). I see this switching often in people when they get mad in the store (customers). I back up and take a breath. It is scary to see this happen in others. So much confusion.

After that session, I wanted for the first time, a nice home and I could see it! Perhaps the dog was the adopted image I saw through. I was trying to match my great aunt's life—trying to get the outer life to match with the inner picture. I feel like I want to throw up physically as I say that. It is now revolting to me.

I am 61 and just beginning my life of peacefulness, quiet inside the head, wanting to do things. My interests are not many, yet I feel like I have been gone in a dream-like world and I am becoming a real person, a healthy person."

(A follow-up: She has purchased her first home.)

Note: Used by permission.

The First and Longest Successful Intergration

This appears as she emailed it to me

April 1, 2014

"My life has improved exponentially, as a result of the integration of my alters. The first thing to develop was that I had continuity in my daily living. There became a time as therapy progressed that I developed a greater sense of self-awareness. As a result of being in therapy with Dr. Earl Flora Psy.D., I had grown into ONE mind. My sense of time became linear. I no longer had missing time. I had become victorious of being in the present moment, because there was a great fullness added to my life. My actions resulted in consequence, and I had a sure footedness to each step I took. My life did not become perfect, yet along the way I learned new coping skills. I do not dissociate or make new alters to deal with my daily issues. There have been times; I missed certain parts of myself, even though I know now that they are aspects of my personality. Over the years since therapy ended in 1998, the integrations have held. Moreover, I no longer seek suicide because the utter confusion has ended. It is not that I feel better because others accept me; it is because I now have knowledge about myself."

Note: Used by permission.

A Married Nurse and Mother

"The first time I met Dr. Flora I had already been struggling with my work and home life. My husband had started researching my symptoms at home and asked me to see a psychologist. I was newly remarried with two young boys, living in a new state and still new in my career as a nurse. I truly thought I was having a hard time adjusting and depressed. I looked up psychologists in my area, I saw that he took our insurance; so I called and made an appointment. I was able to see him that afternoon after work.

The very first visit I felt comfortable with him and felt like it would be good to work with him on my depression issues. After a few visits of Dr. Flora listening to my problems he asked me a few questions that changed everything. "Do I lose time?

Earl Flora

One of the problems at home was that my husband would tell me I had conversations that I would swear I didn't. He would come home mad and ready to argue and I would be excited to see him. When I realized his confusion he asked me to look at my text messages I had written just an hour before. I could not figure out when or why I had written such viscous things to my husband. The answer was, 'Yes.' I thought it was due to the stress of everything being so new.

The other question was, 'Do I talk to myself?' I can't recall my exact answer, but I remember what I was thinking. 'Yes I do, so do a lot of people!' He asked me to give him examples and I did my best. If I remember right, during the next appointment Dr. Flora asked me how much I knew about Dissociative Identity Disorder (DID). I explained what I knew which was very little. He then told me something that changed my life.

He told me that he believed DID was what I was actually suffering from. I was shocked. All I could think was, 'Is this guy crazy?' I went home and told my husband and he, too, felt this doctor might be the wrong doctor to work with at that point. I went to my sister and she also found this hard to believe and explained that a lot of people do not even recognize this as a true disorder. I was nervous when I went back to Dr. Flora because I felt he would not be able to help me with what was 'really' going on.

I continued to work with Dr. Flora because he was able to make me see that I really was suffering from DID. The process was long; he needed to get to know everyone. He did this by just talking to me. I would switch just by him asking if someone else would talk to him. I knew this was real when he did this and when he began to tell me about things that were going on in my life or that had happened in the past that I know "I" didn't tell him.

Then They Were One

My alters were all named the same name. They all began to trust our doctor. He never made decisions for me; he only gave views and opinions. I understood that in order to get control over myself and my life I needed to help in joining my alters. When I made the decision to start this process, Dr. Flora performed what he calls an 'As If' ceremony.

I will do my best explaining the process and how I actually felt. In a quiet and calm setting in his office I close my eyes. The first thing I physically feel is beginning to take the hand of a person that looks like me. I can't say it's a comfortable feeling at first; the other person seems apprehensive holding my hand loosely. I just hold her hand tighter. Dr. Flora asks us to embrace. We hold one another and it feels as if this warm light is shining on us.

In joining some of the alters this part was different. Some of these alters I wanted to hold and felt as if I was saying goodbye. Others I was scared of holding and felt like I was holding my breath waiting for it to be over. Dr. Flora states, 'Processing all of (your) our life events to the present as if we were never separated, removing all hurt, pain and suffering, causing it to come out into the form of a vapor above (you) me, going up into the atmosphere into outer space never to be seen again,(thus) allowing time to heal all wounds.' During this part I sometimes was able to see in my head things that I had forgotten in the past as well as things I did that I never knew I did. The best way I can describe it would be to say it was like a quick flash. Only certain pictures would stand out enough for me to remember. Soon I would forget them, like dreams that you remember that morning and throughout the day you forget the specifics.

Going on in his 'As If' ceremony he would continue talking, 'Fill (any) the void left by the removal of the hurt, pain and suffering with the love of God the Father, God the Son and God the Holy Ghost that passes all understanding. What God has joined together let no one take apart.' At this point I am feeling the overwhelming feeling of the Lord as you may, when you pray, tearful in a good way. He continues, 'As the light goes up you open your eyes (as the name of the core).'

Earl Flora

When I open my eyes, there is Dr. Flora, sitting there calmly and quietly, patiently waiting for me to speak. When it was over, I did not feel any different. Everything I felt during the 'As If' ceremony, the emotion, was gone. I would leave the office feeling pretty close to the same as when I got there, like nothing ever happened.

The nights after the appointment, though, would be filled with dreams. The dreams felt so real that I would ask my husband if this had ever happened or did I dream it. Many times the things I dreamed about were things of the past that my sister or mother would confirm for the most part. Every time we joined an alter the dreams would happen for about a week. Although there were emotions during the 'As If' ceremony, there was never physical or emotional pain.

The change in me was gradual. Nothing was obvious overnight. But slowly I became more accountable at work. My husband started understanding what I was dealing with and was full of support. He started to see a change in me as well. Not losing time in my life was the most helpful outcome. From the time I met Dr. Flora to the time he told me I no longer needed to be seen was over a year's time.

Once all alters were joined, I still needed to see him for some life skills counseling. Because all alters were joined, there were times that I had to deal with things and I no longer knew how. My old way was to switch and I could no longer do that, so it was like certain things were new to me all over again.

Now, I am still happily married, raising our children. I have obtained my bachelor's degree in psychology. I am now in a graduate program to become a mental health counselor, eventually leading to a doctoral program and becoming a Psy.D. like Dr. Flora. I want to help people using the technique he used on me.

Not enough professionals believe that this is a real disorder, which in turn means some people are either not being treated properly or not at all. I believe in this disorder, I believe it is curable and I want to help people the way I was helped."

Note: Used by permission.

Then They Were One

A Middle-aged Married Mother Approaching the End of the Intergration Process on Becoming Whole

I never thought I was not "whole," just maybe a little crazy. After surviving child molestation, being a risky, tumultuous teenager and a depressed, unfulfilled adult until I was over 40, I thought I would always felt like an outsider in my own body. It's hard to describe to an outsider how you can feel like you're not even in your own body at times…I never understood it…I just "played dumb" a lot of times by saying things like "I don't remember that" or "Could you refresh my memory?" But you get to the point that you can't rely on that any longer without believing that you have the worst memory in the world or that you really are losing your marbles.

I could never figure out what made me different. At times I just tried to accept that everyone was this way but when I would try to talk to friends about it, they thought I was just kidding around all the time. I wanted to know if they listened to the voices in their heads and if they ever told them the things I was always hearing…I'm surprised no one sent me to the insane asylum long ago!

The Many Pieces of MY Mind
- Sally
- Audrey
- Richard
- Linda
- Butch
- Amy
- Marie
- Steve
- Angel
- Shelley
- Mary
- HER

Because I was always joking around about this, everyone thought I was a real clown. It did not take me long to realize humor would serve me well when I could not remember what I should

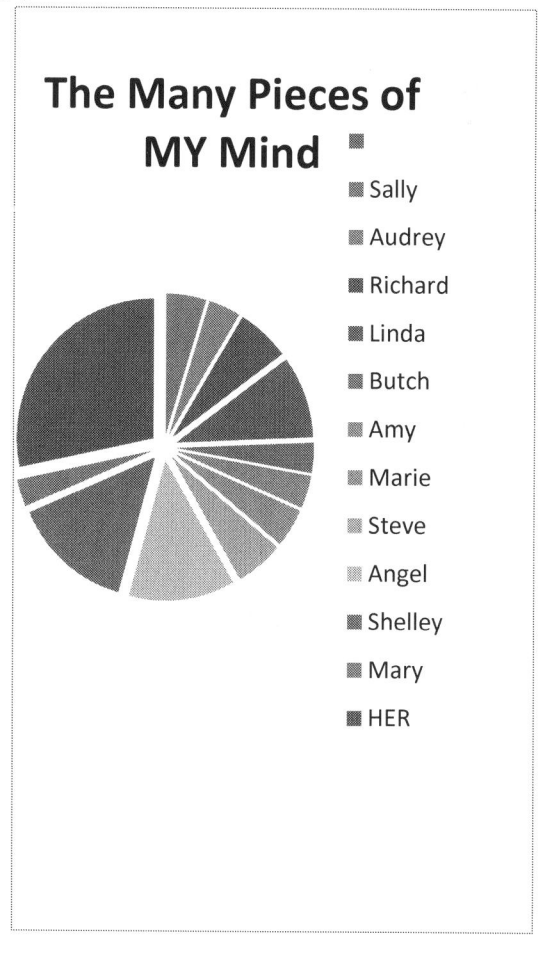

Earl Flora

have.

Sometimes now I look back and I wonder how I survived all these years but when you don't know any different, you just keep on going. There were times, when I was at my lowest and listening to the voices in my head, that I almost ended my life. I mean I guess I was happy but not "whole" as I know what that means now. I just knew something was missing.

I know it was by the grace of God that I found Dr. Flora. Since I have been his patient I have been going through a total transformation. Many of my friends see it and comment that I seem happier and I am. I can't *not* be happy. Finally the pieces are falling into place. Slowly and surely I am being made whole and now I *know* what that means! Dr. Flora has been my salvation and his technique for bringing someone "together" as he has done with me is nothing short of miraculous.

He asked me what it felt like to bring my alters together with the real me. I've been thinking of how to describe it. If you have never been "different" then you will not know. If you think the way you are is "normal" then finding out you are part of a very small minority who are not "normal" compared to everyone else, it is very overwhelming.

I thought everyone heard the voices in their head. I heard many different voices, different ages and even different sexes. There were times, especially if I was having a particularly stressing time that I would get a terrible headache because they were all screaming or arguing at once, all telling me to do something different.

I can remember telling my husband if I did not sleep well that "I couldn't get my mind quiet." He would jokingly ask me what that meant. How do you explain to your spouse that you hear all these voices without appearing to be very insane?

That was truly the hardest part of my existence because I felt if I told anyone what that really meant, that I was hearing children and adults yelling at each other in my mind, they would have had me committed. Therefore, I just laughed, shrugged it off and would say that I had a lot on my mind *(not that I had many people in my mind!)*.

With Dr. Flora's guidance, we determined there were approximately 25 'others' sharing my physical body. They were different ages and some of the opposite sex. The first time Dr. Flora wanted to 'join' one of my alters to the real me, I was scared to death! I mean what was I supposed to feel? You've just been told there are all these other personalities in your head and to heal thyself they each had to be absorbed by my mind. This seemed impossible.

I was still in shock and somewhat in denial with the diagnosis. Was I ready to go this route? Why couldn't I just continue living the way I was? I was so used to it I could just keep doing it, right? No, I could not do it any longer.

After discussing this further with Dr. Flora I realized that I was not *living,* I just existed. This was the only way to truly enjoy life and he assured me it would be painless and I would be much happier. It still seemed daunting and I wondered if it would validate all the years of my thinking I was insane or would this push me over the edge? Could I handle it?

I was very scared and told Dr. Flora that I was. He assured me I was ready and he would let the alters decide if they wanted to stay together and not be separate from my mind. He also assured me it would be painless because he would take away the hurt and pain so that I only received the memories without the negative feelings. He said his technique had worked hundreds of times on other DIDs. OK, then with all this support, I had to do it. I wanted a better life.

Earl Flora

That first joining was almost two years ago now. We've come a long way since then. He was so right about taking away the hurt and pain. I have been able to recall memories from my past without having to relive the pain associated with any bad memories. I feel that becoming whole and gaining all my memories back has literally saved my life. The times that I was at my lowest and darkest are very faint memories now, all thanks to Dr. Flora's technique.

I've read up on DID and learned that some practitioners make a person recall and relive those painful memories and experiences each time an alter is brought back into the conscious mind of the individual and how much pain and sadness that causes the patient. I cannot imagine having to go through that. There's a reason we created those alters in the first place, to disassociate a terrible time in our lives and be able to still function on a daily basis. If I had to relive the hurt, pain or suffering associated with those bad times each time an alter was joined to me, I do not think I would have ever continued treatment. I would have listened to those dark entities that told me everyone, including myself, would be better off if I were dead. I cannot imagine how that must feel, to be overwhelmed all at once with sad, horrible, painful feelings associated with potentially harmful memories.

I am so happy I found Dr. Flora and am starting my healing process in a very loving and gentle environment. I am the happiest I have ever been in my life and I cherish the good memories I have gained. The negative feelings associated with certain memories do not feel as ominous as I think they might have felt if I had not disassociated. As I understand it, we sometimes create these alters to deal with dark times in our lives. Knowing more about these times in my own life, I do not think I had the means to deal with the trauma and emotions that come out of these events.

When these 'bad time alters' are joined with the conscious, I first only feel peace and relief, but as time goes on, the hurtful memories are revealed a little at a time. Not everyone has the same experience. Some DID patients can immediately recall those life events. I, on the other hand, seem to absorb the bad and hurtful life events slowly. I picture my mind as a giant mixing bowl.

Then They Were One

As each alter is added to the mix, my bowl fills up. Like in a recipe when you 'fold in the flour,' my mind seems to "fold in the hurtful memories and feelings" a little at a time. I picture a never-ending conveyor belt filled with memories and experiences. As they are folded into the bowl and as the mix becomes larger, the mind releases the batter (the memories) onto the cooking sheet to be absorbed into my being at my own pace. This is done slowly so my mind does not implode and cause me to create other alters or to completely shut down. Perhaps that is my mind still protecting me.

There have been some alters that were harder to join and Dr. Flora could always tell because I would start to cry after the 'As If' ceremony as hurtful memories started pouring in. He would immediately perform the 'As If' ceremony again. I think my mind is smarter than I ever thought it was. It innately knows my emotional barometer, knows how I would react to certain memories and still tries to protect me.

I am beginning to feel 'whole' and I know I have a lot more therapy in my future but I am not afraid of it anymore. I'm not afraid of the future, I look forward to it…I'm not ashamed of what I am…I embrace it and I want to help others who are suffering in silence, not realizing there is help for them, that it doesn't have to be painful.

To everyone reading about Dr. Flora's technique, please believe me when I tell you that I truly believe in it and I will always credit Dr. Flora for saving my life. For years, I thought I would be better off dead because I felt so useless and depressed. Now, with his help and guidance, I look forward to growing old and to ONE day meeting my grandchildren. I now feel I have everything to live for.

My mind is so much quieter than it used to be, I function so much better and I can recall memories from my childhood and truly revel in those good times. I can actually remember the infant and toddler years of my own 16-year-old daughter that were lost and I am a better mother, wife and daughter. Thank you Dr. Flora for helping me become more of me and for helping me realize that I'm as "normal" as anyone else. For what is "normal" anyway?"

Earl Flora

Note: Used by permission.

(Note: As of this date she is completely together, however it will take another 6 months before it can presume she will more than likely not be able to create any new alters.)

CHAPTER FIFTEEN - INTERVIEW, DIAGNOSIS AND TREATMENT

I decided to leave my interview technique to the end of the book I feel it's more important that the reader becomes acquainted with my particular—maybe to some of my readers, peculiar—style.

There is a pattern but how it is played out varies from client to client. There is nothing different about the beginning of my evaluation. I have a standard protocol to rule out DID with every new client at the onset. After introductions, I explain I follow a standard procedure where I ask various questions. After that they can tell me how they think I may be able to help them.

I administer a standard Mental Status and Behavioral Evaluation. They have already filled out a problem check list, which I use as a reference. Everything is standard, as taught in graduate school, until I get to the hallucination questions (which I will elaborate on a little later).

Interview/Diagnosis

- Introduction
- Explain the limits of confidentiality.
- Review their intake questionnaire with problem list.
- Make initial mental status and behavioral evaluation.
- Record background information, reasons for seeking therapy, strengths, weaknesses and treatment goals.
- Perform appropriate testing as indicated:
  * Beck Depression Scale
  * Mini-Mental State Examination
  * Millon Clinical Multiaxial Inventory III, (MCMI III)
  * INDIVIDUAL DISSOCIATIVE IDENTITY DISORDER CHECK LIST (IDICL), (See in Index.)
  * EXTERNAL DISSOCIATIVE IDENTITY CHECK LIST OBSERVED BY OTHERS (EDICLOBO) (See in Index.)
  * CHILD DISSOCIATIVE CHECKLIST (CDC) (See in Index.)

- Ascertain the correct diagnosis only after talking to an alter, other than the ONE who first presented herself/himself, face to face. This establishes the DID diagnosis.

Treatment (not necessarily in this order):

- If DID, begin to develop rapport.
- Promise to always be honest and never do anything that will hurt them.
- Promise to take the hurt, pain and suffering away, but keep their life experiences.
- Promise no true alter goes away or dies.
- Promise to do everything I can to protect them and ensure the safety of all personalities, even if I have to limit the abilities of others inside that might want to harm the system
- Be careful about setting more restrictions than absolutely necessary, because if they are genuine alters I will have difficulty winning their trust and getting them to agree to join.
- Promise I will never force them to give up their separateness.
- Identify the core personality.
- Establish an internal co-therapist.
- Answer questions to reduce anxiety.
- Explain dissociation advantages/disadvantages.
- Set ground rules.
- Set "complete integration" as the primary treatment goal.
- Begin building confidence within the core personality. (Note: I feel it is counterproductive to empower various alters that may be higher functioning. Rather, I focus on empowering the core by limiting the time lesser alters spend in the conscious mind (e.g., in executive control). I focus on keeping the core upfront in every session so she/he plays an ever increasing-role in the system.
- Identify alters by age at birth, age now and function as therapy progresses.

- As therapy develops offer a "trial fusion with a volunteer alter" (see below.)
- Minimize contact with other alters except the core and the "co-therapist."
- Set up suggestions that prevent oppositional alters from blocking me (e.g., *"No one can block me on the count of three, one, two, three!"*). Said with authority, it works 99 percent of the time. With stronger protectors it will take longer to gain their cooperation but there is always that exception.
- Set up the same block to prevent anyone from interfering with my ability to communicate with the co-therapist (e.g., I say, *"No one can block my co-therapist (CT) on the count of three, one, two, three!"*).
- Continue to deal with current therapeutic issues, always working toward final fusion with a variation on the theme.
- Encourage them to keep a notebook handy so alters can send messages to me between sessions. This is invaluable in speeding up the therapy.

Details:

"**Hallucinations**" are the lynchpin question in ruling out DID or making the diagnosis. It is all in how you ask the question (Note: I do not believe DID voices that communicate with me are auditory hallucinations.):

- I ask the usual, *"Do you ever see things other people say they can't see?"* Most of the time they quickly answer *"No."*
- Then I ask, *"Do you ever hear voices talking when no one is around?"* Again most of the time I get a quick *"No."*
- Then I ask, *"Do you ever hear your thoughts OUT LOUD?"* (Caps for emphasis only.)

If they are not DID, they usually answer *"No"* quickly. (Note: On rare occasions a DID will answer *"No"* quickly. If there are other signs, I will be able to tease it out later in the interview.) In most DID cases they hesitate.

They may ask, *"What do you mean?"*

I explain, *"Some people are able to hear their thoughts inside their heads out loud, just like you are hearing my voice talking to you now. Some people are able to carry on conversations with these voices. You might call it talking to yourself."*

I will get a variety of answers, such as, *"Well, yes,"* or *"Yes, but I hear my own voice inside my head. Doesn't everybody?"* I usually interpret that response as, *"I'm not crazy or demon possessed."*

If they think by admitting they are hearing their thoughts out loud I will think they are crazy, they will deny hearing their thoughts out loud.

If I am fairly certain they do hear their thoughts out loud, whether they admit it or not, I explain there are two types of voices individuals hear. One is psychotic and out of touch with reality. The other voices are the result of a developmental phenomenon called dissociation and are not psychotic. I further explain the psychotic voices are usually command voices telling the person to do bad things to themselves or to other people. The individual cannot carry on a conversation with them. (Note: I realize that a DID can have persecutor voices telling them negative things to hurt or kill themselves, but at this stage, I do not make reference to them unless the client brings that to my attention. I deal with that when it comes up.)

I further ask:

- *"Can you describe how you process your thoughts?"*
- *"Have you ever considered that some of your thoughts are not really yours or you don't have any idea where they come from?"*
- If they admit that they hear their thoughts out loud, at some point I tell them, *"Well, since you can hear your thoughts out loud, this may sound crazy but I'm actually talking past you and addressing the voices inside your head. I'm asking, 'Will any of those voices answer a question for me?'"*
- Then I ask, *"Will you tell me what, if anything, you heard in your mind when I asked, 'Will any of the voices answer a question for me?'"*
- If they are hearing voices they usually spontaneously say what they heard, either *"yes," "no"* or *"maybe."* Any answer will confirm that they are dissociative. (Note: Usually by this time, I am at the end of the initial interview and schedule the next session.)

However, as I stated above, I never make the diagnosis until I actually speak to an alter who has come into executive control of the body and is speaking directly to me!

In every situation, this is a critical time in establishing a therapeutic alliance and more so in DID cases. I have, through sad experience, discovered it is not in the clients' best interest to spring a DID diagnosis on them in the first session unless they have been in therapy for many years with multiple diagnoses and report no real progress. In addition if they have had the diagnosis suggested to them by another therapist, then I will consider asking them a few questions relating to DID systems. If that piques their interest, I suggest they allow me to ask them a series of questions that will help us rule out certain possibilities. With their consent, I go over the INDIVIDUAL DISSOCIATIVE IDENTITY CHECK LIST (IDICL) questions. (See in APPENDIX.)

At the initial interview, if a minor is the identified client, I have the parent come in first to provide significant data. If the parent presents strong DID evidence, I will consider asking the parent to answer the questions on the CHILD DISSOCIATIVE IDENTITY CHECK LIST (CDC). (See in APPENDIX.) I may ask the client the same questions or wait until a later session.

Obviously I have no hard-and fast -rule when, if at all, I will use the CDC. It is left up to my clinical judgment.

Even though I have described a system, I do not really have a fixed track I run on once I finish the mental status and behavioral interview. I more or less take my cue from my clients. However, let me make it very clear that I am committed to complete integration from the moment they are diagnosed DID. I realize that many DID clients drop out of therapy before final fusion, for one reason or another, but even then they will be functioning at a higher level. There are major idiosyncratic problems peculiar to DID clients.

It is my clinical judgment DID clients cannot understand the concept of being of "ONE MIND" at this juncture in the process, any more than I as a mono (e.g., an individual who cannot compartmentalize) can understand how I could possibly survive with a divided mind.

So what is the ethical thing to do? First of all, *"Do no harm."* I do not want to create a problem for which I have no immediate solution. To be even more honest they cannot understand they are not functioning like everybody else. They think everybody hears their thoughts out loud. They cannot understand they share the conscious mind with various earlier life experiences (e.g., alters). They believe they are individual human beings with separate bodies. (More than one alter has at first called me a quack or said I was crazy. I love to hear that because it only validates the diagnosis further.)

In the second session, I usually do the following with variations:

- To get a base line of DID symptoms, I administer the IDICL early and at the end of therapy to validate progress.
- I ask, *"Is there a volunteer inside who will be my "Co-therapist"* (CT), *who will always be honest with me, as I will be with all of you?"* After I get a volunteer I ask, *"Is it all right if I refer to you as CT?"* (Note: Early on in my practice I identified this alter as subconscious [SC]. Later I realized this excluded my ability to access the "True Subconscious Mind," as I would do after inducing a formal trance with a non-dissociative client. This is a concept I first learned many years ago from others who used other terms to identify this helper persona. As mentioned before, in almost all cases it turned out that this alter was a young child who wanted to please me.)
- Again, from a procedural perspective, I never induce a formal trance to establish the diagnosis because they are in a perpetual state of self-hypnosis. All I have to do is direct them, as if I had induced a trance, and they respond.
- To avoid creating false memories, in most situations, when accessing an alter, I am careful not to ask leading questions. I simply say, *"Close your eyes and tell me what you see."*
- Whenever the core complains about a strange feeling or interference in her/his life I say, *"Close your eyes and you will see who or what is behind the feelings."* I have to be flexible and go with the flow all the time.
- Along the above lines, by not inducing a formal trance, I partially avoid the criticism that I am creating the dissociative phenomenon. I might add here, even if someone agreed to be the subject of an experiment to create DID in them that could not include a lifelong history, observed by significant others, needed to fully establish DID. (Note: I have been fortunate enough to have been able to validate lifelong histories through parents or spouses of DID clients. (Note: It is not within the scope of this work to analyze or critique those findings.)

- Answer any questions about the therapeutic goal of "ONE MIND."
- Continue to explain the natural origin of dissociation as one of the innate survival techniques that animal and human beings come into the world with. This is the ability of the newborn, whether human or animal, to internalize, in the face of perceived danger. I describe the opossum's "playing dead" as an example of dissociation in the animal kingdom.
- I explain that everyone dissociates on a continuum. Some very intelligent people are able to do it so well they exclude other coping mechanisms. (Note: It has been my experience that a higher-than-average IQ is essential to form DID. This is not to say all above-average IQ people develop DID. Obviously IQ is not the deciding factor. I believe it is found in the DNA since I have worked with intergenerational parent, child, grandparent DID clients.)
- Continuing my goal of normalizing my DID clients, I explain how the majority of the human population dissociates when they tune someone out when they're concentrating on a TV program and never hear someone address them. They dissociate when they visualize a graphic picture an author is describing in text on paper or a screen. They can dissociate by daydreaming, internally visualizing via their imagination, or ultimately dissociating when put in a hypnotic trance. These are but a few examples of various instances where the majority of people utilize dissociation. I'm sure others can come up with many more examples to help the DID begin to comprehend the concept. I explain how they will still be able to dissociate, in a normal fashion, as they develop other adaptive coping skills in the course of their therapy.
- I explain how their ability to dissociate, to the exclusion of other defense mechanisms, has been beneficial in their survival to this point, but now it has become a liability. I explain how it keeps them from having the ability to draw upon a lifetime of experiences, both good and not so good, in the form of collective wisdom. As I paraphrase a famous quotation, "Those who are ignorant of their past are doomed

to repeat the same mistakes." "How many times should ONE have to touch a hot stove, to not have to touch it again?"
- I explain the concept of "synergism" by holding up both of my hands with the fingers and thumbs extended and separated. I say, *"Visualize this as a divided mind. Extended like this you could easily break off each finger with very little effort, ONE by ONE. But now as I bring both hands together, interlocking the fingers tightly, synergistically it will take more force than any ONE person can exert to break them apart, because the whole is greater than the sum of the parts!"*
- I continue to compare how they see the world through a telescope by joining my hands together as in prayer, holding them up in front of my face to form a small circle that I look through straight at them. (Note: Keep in mind many of the alters listening to me are children, so the simpler the illustrations the better.) From their viewpoint, they can see the small hole formed by my hands. I then expand the circle so they can compare just how much of the picture (e.g., their life) they are missing by staying separate.
- What does it mean to come together? I say, *"No ONE possessing conscious life experience dies. No ONE with "conscious life experience" goes away. All you experience is giving up the hurt, pain and suffering. By giving up the negative feelings, you actually gain valuable life experiences previously hidden from your conscious mind. You never lose your life experiences, which make you who you are. All of us are an accumulation of our life experiences. It's no more complicated than that. In addition to giving up the pain and suffering, you are brought into the mainstream of life from which you had been excluded."*

(Note: At this point I am sure none of them understand the concept of Oneness, but I say it for anyone who can. Actually I do not believe it is completely understood until their final fusion has ended the separateness, and there has been sufficient time to coalesce the mind before a true understanding is possible.

As the therapy progresses and the core gains more and more life experience, her/his life will start making more and more sense. Things previously said, that made no sense, start to take on more meaning. Just because some or all alters cannot understand the concept is no reason for me to second guess them.)

I explain, *"When one of you agrees to join the core, gone is the alienation, the separation, the loneliness and the rejection. By giving up the pain and suffering you are immediately part of the life experience and participate as one mind in all future decisions."*

I explain, *"In the past, the subconscious mind decided the hurt feelings accompanying certain life events were so powerful that the system could not survive unless they were separated from the ability of the conscious mind to retrieve them. So in a still unknown procedure,* (Note: It is not in the purview of this book to explain how the mind accomplishes switching.) *the subconscious mind walled off entire events, along with their hurt, pain and suffering, from the conscious mind. The problem created was time could not do its job because 'time stopped' once the amnestic barriers were erected. Since time stopped it could not continue the healing process."*

Then They Were One

- I say, *"To remedy this problem and free your mind we will remove the barrier, which is the negative affect, by removing the hurt, pain and suffering without making you relive the pain associated with the experience and instantly allow time to heal the wound "as if" you were never separate. We'll do this simply with talking therapy alone."* (Note: Assuming no co-morbidity.)
- Once we can agree on the goal of final fusion, we establish just which personality will be the designated "core" into which all other personalities will be integrated. Usually it is the presenting personality but not always as this current personality is usually less traumatized. Next establish what name she/he will be using.
- Then I begin what others call "mapping." I simply call it what it is in plain English, "identifying the various alters." This is accomplished by asking my co-therapist to tell me how many individuals she/he sees inside. I then record the number in my session notes and on the inside of the manila folder in which I keep the client's session notes. I find this a handy place to record the different alters' names, etc., since I usually keep this open while in session for easy reference and record additional data as it is revealed. (I admit it doesn't look very neat, but it works for me. To each his/her own.)
- As each alter is identified, I ask the following questions:
  a. *"What is your name?"* Don't be surprised if they say they do not have a name. Identify them by the following.
  b. *"How old are you?"*
  c. *"How old were you when you were born?"* (Note: Now, if that's not a crazy question to ask a non-DID, I've never heard one. But you will be surprised when they quickly answer 3, 7, 17, 25 or whatever age in a matter-of-fact way. This is invaluable information, as it establishes not only the chronological body age when they were created, but it establishes just how much time they have spent in the conscious mind. This lets me know just how much influence/power they possess.

d. *"What do you do?"* This establishes whether they have a specific function or not.
   e. *"What is your earliest memory?"* This establishes just what caused the split and establishes the level of the trauma.
- As they are integrated I enter that date next to their name/identity.
- I avoid at all cost giving alters anymore time in the conscious mind than necessary to effect integration as this increases their ability to control the situation.
- I avoid naming the alters, instead addressing them by their function.
- I respect every true alter for the responsibilities they have, especially the protector alters as they have trouble trusting you and are not used to being liked. I work hard at being patient with them. It takes time for them to accept me as someone who is actually taking away the hurt. In the beginning, they may not be very pleased as one by one the alters cease to be seen separately.
- A technique I employ to reduce the internal anxiety as the integration proceeds is to ask the alter who is missing various other alters, *"Can you see so and so* (e.g., the core mentioned by name)?" If they answer yes, I say, *"Walk over to her and just take her hand and you will feel the alters presence within (*I say *her name).*" Say it with confidence, not halfheartedly.
- In every case they say something like, *"You are right. She's not dead; she's part of* (the core mentioned by name)." This has at least three positive effects. It increases the system's trust in the therapist, reduces their anxiety and eases the path to further alters wanting to give up the loneliness of their separateness and integrate.
- Avoid power struggles whenever possible. If the alter is blocking or otherwise sabotaging another alter during therapy, you'll need to place some type of limitations on him/her. (See sections on SITUATIONS TO AVOID in CHAPTER ELEVEN.)

- As integration continues, not too early on so as not to discourage the core, I ask the subconscious mind, *"Will you calculate what percentage of the total life the core personality possesses?"* From that point on with each new integration I ask for an update. This can be a positive or a negative to the core depending on whether the combined core sees the glass half full or half empty. Of course I have no way to validate the percentages, but nevertheless, I use the figures to be my mile markers to the finish line.
- As with any other client populations, I have our successes and my "not-so successes" to coin a phrase. I say "not-so successes" to emphasize the fact that to whatever extent they are integrated when they drop out is that much more time the core personality can stay in the conscious mind and hopefully function at a higher level.
- So as not to despair, I have to remember I can only help those who seek my help. I must remember, in the case of DID, there is a multitude of personalities who can sabotage the therapy for those who seek my help. That's why it is essential that I establish a strong bond with both the core personality and the subconscious mind, if final fusion is to be achieved.
- I see most of my DID clients only once every seven days. I set this as the standard which is, in effect, boundary setting. I tell them in times of crisis I am available 24/7, but they should only call me after office hours if it is an emergency. My secret weapon is my office-manager wife. She sleeps with the office phone and is available 24/7.
- I ask my clients to keep a small spiral notebook nearby at all time so other alters can write to me during the week. Older alters often write for the small children who cannot write. It is very interesting to get printed notes with misspelled words from a young child alter asking for help. This really accelerates the therapeutic process. I read their journal at the beginning of each session. If a client refuses to keep a journal, I do not make a big deal out of it. However, if a protector alter is tearing up the pages, then I will say something like, *"The alter who is destroying the journal will not be able to see the journal as long as he wants to destroy*

it, on the count of three, one, two, three." *About* 99 percent of the time whatever I say works. (Note: I still haven't been able to figure out why counting to three works even with raising my two normal sons, but it does. The only thoughts I have are at the starting line in some field competitions. They say one for the money, two for the show, three to get ready and four to go. But I never got to four.)

- Finally, I try to give as much information as needed to answer their questions but not so much that it increases their anxiety. I am reminded, while testifying in a MPD's child-custody case, of the judge's response to the opposing counsel's question to me, "*Dr. Flora, will you please explain what Multiple Personality Disorder is?*" Before I could answer the presiding judge spoke up, "*How do you expect Dr. Flora to explain the inexplicable?*" So my advice to myself and to anyone who might be interested is a version of the KISS method; Keep It Simple so I don't look Stupid!
- From this point on you are pretty much on your own to use whatever I have been using successfully in your own style. I have attempted to give the reader as complete a picture of the "whys and wherefores" of the "As If" technique in as short a space as possible. I make no guarantees, all I can say is "*It works for me.*" I hope you can take away something that will make your work easier, more rewarding and beneficial for all your DID clients/patients.

A side bar: I never underestimate the power of the mind!

I am completely amazed by the power of the mind to give up the negative affect and join the parts in the blink of an eye, while at the same time process their life experiences "as if" they were never separate and keep them in chronological order at the same time. Why they are not all jumbled up is for minds smarter than mine to figure out. (Note: Some memories are instantly integrated, others are integrated during dreams and still others are integrated gradually.

There does not seem to be any set pattern. But in the end, all memories appear to finally be integrated.)

CHAPTER SIXTEEN - POSTLUDE

After getting this far in the book, if I sounded frustrated at times, I apologize if it offended anyone. On the other hand, it was this energy identified as "frustration" that provided the enthusiasm to invest years of trial and error to finally discover the techniques that work and present them in this book. We cannot change the past but we can influence the future. I'm not in the blame game but if there is blame, let's lay it where it belongs for whatever the reason: *"If the student failed to learn, the professor failed to teach."*

Believe it or not, this isn't rocket science. I am an advocate for all those who suffer with DID. This little book has been a work in progress for the past 27 years in the hopes that others less knowledgeable will see how simple it is to diagnose and resolve the separateness without re-traumatizing them, on the ONE hand, but on the other hand, how challenging and rewarding it is to get to the point of actually initiating the "As If" ceremony.

I challenge every graduate school dean in every mental health discipline to mandate that part of the curriculum be devoted to teaching how to diagnose and treat DID and to stop ignoring it as too insignificant.

Just because DID is controversial is no reason not to provide every mental health graduate student with the basic techniques, to at least diagnose DID, if not how to resolve it as well.

The challenge, for the future, is for scientists to discover the dominant gene that perpetuates this phenomenon so that it can be prevented either before or soon after birth.

I want to close with my personal testimony: *"Without fear of contradiction, I can honestly say, finally joining the last alter and being present at the rebirth of an individual suffering from DID have been among the most rewarding and humbling experiences of my life."*
Earl W. Flora, Psy.D.

Earl Flora

Then They Were One

APPENDIX

INDIVIDUAL DISSOCIATION IDENTITY CHECK LIST

Name: _____ AGE: ____ Date: ___/___/___ Interviewer: _____

FINISH/START

1. ____ ____ Do you ever feel worthless?
2. ____ ____ Do you experience frequent headaches?
3. ____ ____ Have you ever come home with groceries you don't remember buying?
4. ____ ____ Do you find yourself wearing clothes you don't remember putting on?
5. ____ ____ Do you find that time goes past very fast at times?
6. ____ ____ Do you ever hear voices talking outside your head, when no ONE is there?
7. ____ ____ Have you ever experienced sudden illnesses that spontaneously remit?
8. ____ ____ Have you ever had difficulty walking?
9. ____ ____ Have you ever experienced blurred or double vision?
10. ____ ____ Do you hear voices carrying on conversations inside your head?
11. ____ ____ Do you have difficulty concentrating or 'space out'?
12. ____ ____ Have you found cuts, burns or bruises on your body and not know how the got there?
13. ____ ____ Do you often think of death or dying?
14. ____ ____ Can you carry on a two-way conversation with yourself?
15. ____ ____ Have you found yourself in a place but not know why you were there?
16. ____ ____ Do you have a rich fantasy life?
17. ____ ____ Are there voices in your head commenting on your behavior?
18. ____ ____ Are you having thoughts that are not your own? They can be intrusive or helpful.
19. ____ ____ Does your handwriting change frequently?
20. ____ ____ Have you ever experienced emotions that make no sense to you?
21. ____ ____ Can you hear your thoughts out loud inside your head?
22. ____ ____ Have you suddenly found yourself in a place and not know how you got there?
23. ____ ____ Have you ever started a project, find it completed, but don't remember finishing it?
24. ____ ____ At school or college, have you gotten test results for tests you didn't remember taking?
25. ____ ____ Are you constantly losing things?
26. ____ ____ Do you find items in your home or personal possessions you don't remember buying?
27. ____ ____ Do people accuse you of saying things you didn't say? Accuse you of lying?
28. ____ ____ Do people accuse you of promising things you know you didn't promise?
29. ____ ____ Have you ever thought there are other people inside your head?
30. ____ ____ Do you have flashbacks/memories suddenly pop up in your mind?
31. ____ ____ Do you have mood swings for no apparent reason?
32. ____ ____ Has anyone ever mistaken you for another person?
33. ____ ____ Is it difficult for you to keep friends?
34. ____ ____ Are you confused at times as to your own identity?
35. ____ ____ Have you ever not recognized the image in the mirror not due to aging?
36. ____ ____ Have you been told you sleepwalk?
37. ____ ____ Do you have difficulty deciding which clothes to put on in the morning?

STARTING DATE ___/___/___ STARTING SCORE _____

FINISHING DATE ___/___/___ FINISHING SCORE _____

(Note: This is not validated as a test to diagnose DID. Use only as a therapeutic tool.)

Earl Flora

EXTERNAL DISSOCIATION IDENTITY CHECK LIST OBSERVED BY OTHERS

Name: _____ Age___ Date: ___/___/___ Interviewer: _____

FINISH/START

1. _____ _____ Frequent unexplained mood swings.
2. _____ _____ Frequent change of clothes.
3. _____ _____ Frequent denial of behavior.
4. _____ _____ Indecisiveness.
5. _____ _____ Poor short-term memory.
6. _____ _____ Procrastinates, (e.g., arrives late or misses appointments.)
7. _____ _____ Self-injurious behavior: cutting, head banging, burning, etc.
8. _____ _____ Suicide attempts.
9. _____ _____ Preoccupied with thoughts of death or dying.
10. _____ _____ Frequent changes in handwriting styles.
11. _____ _____ Prefers ONE food only to deny liking it later.
12. _____ _____ Different allergies that spontaneously remit.
13. _____ _____ Different eyeglasses or contact lens.
14. _____ _____ Strabismus at ONE time but not at another time.
15. _____ _____ Hyperactivity.
16. _____ _____ Changes in voice tone, accent or childlike pronunciation.
17. _____ _____ Occasional spaced-out appearance.
18. _____ _____ Rapid attitude changes.
19. _____ _____ The appearance of another personality, (e.g., acts totally different at times.)
20. _____ _____ Changes in strength, (e.g., able to lift heavy objects, open tight jar lids, but not at other times.)
21. _____ _____ Talks to self, appears to be responding to inner voices.
22. _____ _____ Will refer to self in the plural "We" at times.
23. _____ _____ Out and out lies.
24. _____ _____ May make friends easily, but they do not last long. More of a loner.
24. _____ _____ Childlike behaviors.
25. _____ _____ May have a large collection of stuffed animals or other toys.
26. _____ _____ May like to walk around department stores holding stuffed animals.
27. _____ _____ Preoccupied with toy departments.
28. _____ _____ Furniture/objects are moved around, but the person denies moving them.
29. _____ _____ Complains of frequent headaches.
30. _____ _____ Failure to respond to prior treatments.
31. _____ _____ Multiple diagnoses.
32. _____ _____ Multiple physical complaints.
33. _____ _____ Walks in their sleep.
34. _____ _____ Calls significant others by different names, (e.g., mom, mother, dad, father, etc.)
35. _____ _____ Change in sexual orientation.

STARTING DATE ____/____/____ STARTING SCORE _____

FINISHING DATE ____/____/____ FINISHING SCORE_____

(Note: This has not been validated as a test to diagnose DID. Use only as a tool to help your patient's spouse, parent or significant other gain insight into his/her condition.)

Then They Were One

CHILD DISSOCIATIVE CHECKLIST
(V 3.0 -- 2/90)
Frank W. Putnam, M.D.
Unit on Dissociative Disorders, LDP, NIMH

Date:_____ Age: ____ Sex: M F Identification: _____

Below is a list of behaviors that describe children. For each item that describes your child NOW or WITHIN THE PAST 12 MONTHS, please circle 2 if the item is VERY TRUE of your child. Circle 1 if the item is SOMEWHAT or SOMETIMES TRUE of your child. If the item is NOT TRUE of your child, circle 0.

0 1 2   1. Child does not remember or denies traumatic or painful experiences that are known to have occurred.

0 1 2   2. Child goes into a daze or trance-like state at times or often appears "spaced-out". Teachers may report that he or she 'daydreams' frequently in school.

0 1 2   3. Child shows rapid changes in personality. He or she may go from being shy to being outgoing, from feminine to masculine, from timid to aggressive.

0 1 2   4. Child is unusually forgetful or confused about things that he or she should know, e.g. may forget the names of friends, teachers or other important people, loses possessions or gets lost easily.

0 1 2   5. Child has a very poor sense of time. He or she loses track of time, may think that it is morning when it is actually afternoon, gets confused about what day it is, or becomes confused about when something happened.

0 1 2   6. Child shows marked day-to-day or even hour-to-hour variations in his or her skills, knowledge, food preferences, athletic abilities, e.g. changes in handwriting, memory for previously learned information such as multiplication tables, spelling, use of tools or artistic ability.

0 1 2   7. Child shows rapid regressions in age-level of behavior, e.g. a twelve year-old starts to use baby-talk, sucks thumb or draw like a four year-old.

0 1 2   8. Child has a difficult time learning from experience, e.g. explanations, normal discipline or punishment do not change his or her behavior.

Earl Flora

0 1 2   9. Child continues to lie or deny misbehavior even when the evidence is obvious.

0 1 2   10. Child refers to him or herself in the third person (e.g. as she or her) when talking about self, or at times **insists** on being called by a different name. He or she may also claim that things that he or she did actually happened to another person.

0 1 2   11. Child has rapidly changing physical complaints such as headache or upset stomach. For example, he or she may complain of a headache one minute and seem to forget all about it the next.

0 1 2   12. Child is unusually sexually precocious and may attempt age-inappropriate sexual behavior with other children or adults.

0 1 2   13. Child suffers from unexplained injuries or may even deliberately injure self at times.

0 1 2   14. Child reports hearing voices that talk to him or her. The voices may be friendly or angry and may come from 'imaginary companions' or sound like the voices of parents, friends or teachers.

0 1 2   15. Child has a vivid imaginary companion or companions. Child may insist that the imaginary companion(s) is responsible for things that he or she has done.

0 1 2   16. Child has intense outbursts of anger, often without apparent cause and may display unusual physical strength during these episodes.

0 1 2   17. Child sleepwalks frequently.

0 1 2   18. Child has unusual nighttime experiences, e.g. may report seeing "ghosts" or that things happen at night that he or she can't account for (e.g. broken toys, unexplained injuries).

0 1 2   19. Child frequently talks to him or herself, may use a different voice or argue with self at times.

0 1 2   20. Child has two or more distinct and separate personalities that take control over the child's behavior.

(In Public Domain)

REFERENCES

Abugel J. and Simeon D. (2006). Feeling unreal depersonalization disorder and the loss of the self. Oxford England: Oxford Press, 17.

Bliss, E. L. (1986). Multiple Personality, allied disorders and hypnosis. New York: Oxford University Press.

Brand, B. L., Myrick, A. C., Loewenstein, R. J., Classen, C. C., Lanius, R., McNary, S. W., Pain, C., & Putnam, F. W. (2011). A survey of practices and recommended treatment interventions among expert therapists treating patients with dissociative identity disorder and dissociative disorder not otherwise specified. Psychological Trauma: Theory, Research, Practice, and Policy

Butler, L. D. et al. (July 1996). Hypnotizability and traumatic experience: a diathesis-stress model of dissociative symptomatology. American Journal of Psychiatry 153(7), 42-63.

Carich, M. S. (1991, December). The hypnotic "as if" technique: An example of beyond Adler. Special issue: "On beyond Adler." Individual Psychology Journal of Adlerian Theory, Research and Practice, 47(4), 509-514.

Cheek, D. B. (October 1962). Some applications of hypnosis and ideomotor questioning methods for analysis and therapy in medicine. American Journal of Clinical Hypnosis, 5(2), 92-104.

Coons P.M. (June 1999). Psychogenic or dissociative fugue: a clinical investigation of five cases. Psychological Reports, 84(3 Pt 1). 881-886.

Dell, P. F. (2006). The multidimensional inventory of dissociation (MID): A comprehensive measure of pathological dissociation. Journal of Trauma and Dissociation 7(2), 77-106.

Dell, P. F. (March 2006). A new model of dissociative identity disorder. The Psychiatric Clinics of North America 29, 1-26, vii

Fike, M. (1990, Nov). Considerations and techniques in the treatment of persons with multiple personality disorder. Special Issues: Multiple personality disorder, American Journal of Occupational Therapy, 44(11), 999-1007.

Fine, C. G. (1991, Sep). Treatment stabilization and crisis prevention: Pacing the therapy of the multiple personality disorder patients. Psychiatric Clinics of North America. 14 (3), 661-675.

Flora, E. W. (1988). Tracing the historical development of the diagnosis and treatment of multiple personality disorder in 19th and 20th century North America, Miami Institute of Psychology of the Caribbean Center for Advanced Studies, 203 pages; Dissertation Abstracts International, (University Microfilm No. 8822943)

Gillig, P. M. (2009). Dissociative identity disorder: A controversial diagnosis. Psychiatry. Edgemont (Pa Township) 6(3): 24–29.

Gleaves, D. H., May, M. C., & Cardeña, E. (June 2001). An examination of the diagnostic validity of dissociative identity disorder. Clinical Psychology Review 21(4): 577–608.

Guidelines for treating Dissociative Identity Disorder in adults, Third Revision. (2011). Journal of Trauma & Dissociation 12(2): 188–212.

Kihlstrom, J. F. (2005). Dissociative disorders. Annual Review of Clinical Psychology 1, 227–253.

Kluft, R. P. (1984). Aspects of the treatment of multiple personality disorder. Psychiatric Annals. 14, 51-55.

Kluft, R. P. (1984, April). On treating the older patient with multiple personality disorder: "Race against time" or "make haste slowly?" American Journal of Clinical Hypnosis, 30(4), 257-266.

Kluft, R. P. (1993 June/September). The treatment of dissociative disorder patients: An overview of discoveries, successes, and failures. Dissociation, Progress in the Dissociative Disorders, VI, (2/3), 87-101.

Kohlenberg, R. J., & Tsai, M. (1991). Functional Analytic Psychotherapy: Creating Intense and Curative Therapeutic Relationships. Springer

Kritchevsky, M., Chang, J., & Squire, L. R. (2004). Functional Amnesia: Clinical Description and Neuropsychological Profile of 10 Cases. Learning and Memory 11, 213-226.

Lynn, S. J., Berg, J., Lilienfeld, S. O., Merckelbach, H., Giesbrecht, T., Accardi, M., & Cleere, C. (2012). 14 - Dissociative disorders. In Hersen, M., Beidel, D. C. Adult Psychopathology and Diagnosis. (pp. 497-538). New York, John Wiley & Sons.

Lynn, S. & Rhue, J. W. (1994). Dissociation: clinical and theoretical perspectives. New York, Guilford Press.

MacDonald, K. (2008). Dissociative disorders unclear? Think 'rainbows from pain blows. Current Psychiatry 7(5) 73-85.

Maldonado, J. R., & Spiegel, D. (2008). Dissociative disorders — Dissociative Identity Disorder (Multiple Personality Disorder). In Hales R. E., Yudofsky, S. C., & Gabbard, G. O.; with foreword by Alan F. Schatzberg. The American Psychiatric Publishing Textbook of Psychiatry (5th ed.), (pp. 681-710).

Washington, DC: American Psychiatric Pub.

Prince, M. (1969). The dissociation of a personality (2nd ed.). New York: Greenwood Press. (Original work published in 1906)

Random House Dictionary of the English Language, Unabridged, 1966

Reinders, A. A. (2008). Cross-examining dissociative identity disorder: Neuroimaging and etiology on trial. Neurocase 14(1), 44–53.

Ross, C. A., Helier, S., Norton, R., Anderson, D., Anderson, G., & Barchet, P. (1989). The Dissociative Disorders interview schedule: A structured interview. Dissociation 2(3), 171.

Ross, C. A., Norton, D. R., & Wozney, B. A. (1987). Multiple Personality Disorder: Analysis of 236 cases. In B. G. Braun (Ed.), Proceedings of the Fourth International Conference on Multiple Personality/Dissociative States. 13. Chicago, Illinois: Rush University.

Ross, C. A. (1988, April). Cognitive analysis of multiple personality disorder. American Journal of Psychotherapy, 42(2), 229-239.

Ross, C. A. (1989). Multiple Personality Disorder: Diagnosis, clinical features, and treatment. New York: J. Wiley & Sons.

"Schneiderian first-second-rank systems" Oxford University Press, Oxford Index, http://oxfordindex.oup.com/view/10.1093/oi/authority 20110803100446631

Snyder, C. R., (Ed.) (1999). Coping: The Psychology of What Works. New York, Oxford University Press.

Shapiro, M. K. (1991, July). Bandaging a "broken heart": Hypnoplay therapy in the treatment of multiple personality disorder. American Journal of Clinical Hypnosis, 34(1), 1-10.

Steel, K. H. (1989, September). A model for abreaction with DID and other dissociative disorders. Dissociation, Progress in the Dissociative Disorders, 2(3), 151-159.

Steinberg, M., Rounsaville B., & Cicchetti D. V. (1990). The structured clinical interview for DSM-III-R Dissociative Disorders: Preliminary report on a new diagnostic instrument. The American Journal of Psychiatry 147 (1), 76–82

Thigpen, C. H., & Cleckley, H. M. (1984). On the incidence of multiple personality disorder: a brief communication. The International Journal of Clinical and Experimental Hypnosis, 32, 670101

Vaihinger, H. (1924). First published in England by Routledge & Kegan Paul Ltd., Reprinted (1968). The Philosophy of "As If." London, Translated by Ogden, C. K. (pp. 92-93). New York, Barnes & Noble, Inc.

Van der Kolk, B. A., Van der Hart, O., & Marmar, C. R. (1996). Dissociation and information processing in posttraumatic stress disorder. In B. A. van der Kolk, A. C. McFarlane, & L. Weisaeth. Traumatic stress: The effects of overwhelming experience on mind, body, and society. (pp. 303–327). New York, Guilford Press.

Van Ijzendoorn, M. H., & Schuengel, C. (1996). The measurement of dissociation in normal and clinical populations: Meta-analytic validation of the dissociative experience scale (DES). Clinical Psychology Review 16 (5), 365-382.

Weiten, W. & Lloyd, M. A. (2008). Psychology applied to modern life: Adjustment in the 21st Century, personal explorations workbook. (9th ed.). Independence, KY: Wadsworth Cengage Learning.

Yapko, M. D. (1988). When living hurts, direction for treating depression. (pp. 73-74). New York: Brunner/Mazel.

Zeidner, M. & Endler, N., (Ed.). (1996). Handbook of coping: Theory, research, applications. New York: John Wiley & Sons.

INDEX

"As If", 7, 17, 18, 19, 26, 33, 40, 42, 43, 44, 46, 47, 65, 67, 73, 74, 75, 77, 83, 85, 86, 91, 93, 94, 97, 99, 101, 102, 107, 110, 112, 113, 115, 120, 121, 122, 124, 125, 154, 155
"self-fulfilling prophesy.", 33
137 alters, 49
23 child alters, 54
27 years, 18
35 mm film, 37
35 mm movie film, 37
A 60-year-old female started her period, 101
A basketful of babies, 111
a child's game gone awry, 28
A guy with a sword, 109
A little girl kept moving out of reach, 76
A partial "As If, 75
aborted fetus, 121
abreacting, 41
abreaction, 17, 18, 19, 39, 41, 42, 43, 58, 63, 75, 164
Abreaction, 33, 55
Abugel J, 161
abused, 18
Accardi M, 25
Accardi, M, 163
ACKNOWLEDGMENT, 7
acquired life experiences, 18, 19
actions, 23, 28, 30, 81, 88, 131
adjunct faculty at The College of William & Mary, 16
Adjusting, 18

admonished, 29
age progression, 33
aggressive behavior, 23
Alexandre Bertrand, 23
almost painlessly, 18
alter is hurting the core, 88
Alter/personality, 32
alternative coping techniques, 18
alters, 18, 19, 32, 33, 34, 35, 36, 38, 39, 41, 42, 46, 49, 50, 51, 54, 63, 65, 66, 67, 70, 72, 73, 74, 75, 77, 80, 81, 83, 84, 85, 86, 87, 89, 91, 92, 96, 97, 98, 99, 103, 105, 106, 110, 111, 112, 113, 114, 115, 117, 118, 119, 127, 128, 131, 133, 134, 136, 137, 138, 139, 140, 142, 143, 146, 149, 150, 151, 152, 153
ALTERS CREATING PROBLEMS, 79
ALTERS REFUSING TO JOIN, 74
American Psychiatric Association's 2013 Diagnostic and Statistical Manual of Mental Disorders 5, 27
amnestic, 18, 24, 27, 28, 32, 33, 74, 75, 82, 150
amnestic barriers, 18, 28, 74, 75, 150
an altered state of consciousness, 41, 77, 118
ancient, 23
Anderson, D, 164
Anderson, G, 164
animal magnetism, 23

APPENDIX, 29, 30, 97, 99, 145, 146, 157
As If" ceremony, 42, 46, 47, 73, 75, 83, 85, 86, 91, 93, 94, 101, 102, 107, 110, 112, 113, 115, 120, 121, 122, 125, 155
As If" fusion technique, 17
assimilated, 18, 39, 42, 73, 74
authenticity, 22
awards, 23
bachelor's degree in Bible from the Philadelphia College of Bible (now Cairn University, 17
bachelor's in psychology from Florida International University, 17
Barchet, P, 164
barrier, 18, 27, 28, 32, 33, 82, 96, 151
barrier to be erected, 27
barriers, 18, 37, 54, 68, 74
behaviors, 23, 30, 31, 79, 158
believing, 22, 35, 135
belittled, 28
Berg J, 25
Berg, J, 163
Bible, 17, 23, 24, 71
birth mother, 67
blamed, 60, 81
Bliss, 23, 39, 41, 42, 161
blocking, 28, 63, 90, 92, 143, 152
born, 27, 28, 51, 66, 76, 151
brain functions, 30
Butler, L. D, 161
bypass, 41, 118
camp, 23
cancellation, 60

Cardeña, E, 162
career, 23, 131
caregiver, 28
Carich, M. S., 161
case studies, 19, 41
Caucasian, 42, 49, 51, 53, 79
ceremony, 44
Ceremony, 33, 44, 46
Chang, J, 163
change, 18, 23, 24, 28, 29, 38, 85, 88, 89, 99, 101, 108, 109, 115, 134, 155, 157, 158
Cheek, 31, 161
child custody, 17
child sexual abuse, 17
childhood, 28, 56, 88, 139
Christian, 35, 43, 44, 52
Christians, 70
church-sponsored exorcism, 70
Cicchetti, 165
citing, 19
Classen, C. C, 161
Cleckley, 165
Cleere C, 25
Cleere, C, 163
client, 9, 17, 18, 19, 28, 29, 32, 38, 43, 44, 46, 63, 65, 66, 67, 68, 69, 70, 75, 76, 82, 83, 86, 92, 97, 98, 99, 111, 116, 117, 118, 121, 122, 141, 144, 146, 147, 151, 153
clients,, 18, 67, 148
clinical population, 25
Closely related trauma, 74
Coalescence, 38
Co-conscious, 32
Colin A. Ross, 39, 40
comorbidity, 26

compartmentalized, 28, 32, 36, 65, 77, 88, 92, 103, 112, 115, 116, 120
compartmentalizing, 27, 36
compromised, 23
conference, 29, 41, 70
conscious mind., 28, 32, 45, 83, 84, 89, 93, 94, 108, 119, 149, 150, 151
conscious thought, 29
constant, 18, 38, 59, 62, 83, 92, 97, 99, 114
content, 19, 56, 58
CONTENTS, 11
context, 19, 42, 112
continuum, 27, 148
Coons P.M, 161
coping techniques, 18
core, 16, 19, 32, 33, 41, 42, 44, 45, 46, 47, 49, 50, 51, 52, 54, 67, 73, 74, 76, 82, 83, 84, 85, 86, 87, 88, 90, 91, 93, 94, 97, 98, 99, 100, 101, 104, 105, 108, 109, 111, 114, 116, 118, 119, 121, 123, 129, 133, 142, 143, 147, 150, 151, 152, 153
Core Personality, 33
count of three, 34, 68, 80, 82, 84, 85, 91, 94, 98, 105, 111, 114, 116, 122, 123, 124, 125, 143, 154
CPR, 68
crazy, 22
crib, 28, 80, 99
criteria, 23
criticism, 97, 98, 147
criticized, 16, 28, 83
crying, 23, 28, 90, 128

CT, 31, 32, 51, 65, 66, 68, 69, 73, 76, 79, 80, 84, 86, 94, 101, 104, 105, 118, 143, 147
culprit, 25
Cult induced interjects, 65
daughter, 27, 66, 139
death wish, 83, 84, 85
decreased, 23, 49
dedicated, 18
DEDICATION, 5
defense mechanisms, 27, 28, 61, 148
DEFINITIONS, 27
Dell, P. F, 161
demon, 67, 69, 70, 71, 105, 106, 144
demons, 23, 24, 34, 35, 55, 71, 95, 103, 105
demonstrating, 23
deoxyribonucleic acid (DNA), 27
derivation, 23
desensitized, 18, 39, 42, 74
destroying, 41, 153
Diabetic client, 86
diagnosis, 3, 16, 22, 25, 29, 30, 31, 81, 120, 137, 142, 143, 145, 146, 147, 162
diagnostic, 23, 162, 165
DID Characteristics, 29
DID forensic court cases, 17
DID voices, 30, 143
different voices, 24, 136
differentiate, 30
dilemma, 37, 43, 85, 90, 115
dilute, 41
disappear, 18, 86, 119
disappearance of DID, 25
disciples, 23, 24

DISCLAIMER, 3
discredited, 52
disguise, 19
disintegrated personality, 25
(DSM-5), 26
(DSM-IV-TR), 23
Disney World, 85, 86
Disneyland, 110
disrepute, 23
dissociate, 27, 28, 35, 86, 127, 128, 131, 148
dissociated personalities, 25
Dissociative, 3, 9, 16, 18, 23, 27, 29, 30, 97, 132, 162, 163, 164, 165
Dissociative Identity Disorder (DID), 3, 18, 132
Dissociative Identity Disorder/Multiple Personality Disorder (DID/MPD), 9, 16
dissolve, 18, 104
divorce, 28
doctor of psychology degree with distinction from the Miami Institute of Psychology of the Caribbean Center for Advanced Studies (now Carlos Albizu University)., 17
doctoral dissertation, 17
Dr. Cornelia Wilbur, 25
Dr. Earl Flora's, 9
Dr. Flora, 9, 50, 52, 54, 56, 57, 60, 61, 62, 127, 128, 129, 131, 132, 133, 134, 136, 137, 138, 139, 154
Dr. Frank W. Putnam's, 30

Du Magnétisme Animal en France, 23
duration, 24, 73
Eastern State Hospital, 16, 51
editing, 19
effort, 19, 22, 68, 117, 124, 149
Egyptians, 23
eliminate, 17, 105
Ellenberger, 23, 24, 25
Ellenberger,, 23, 24, 25
embodiment, 24, 67
emotional, 33, 54, 55, 56, 57, 58, 73, 112, 134, 139
emotions, 33, 39, 42, 53, 54, 58, 59, 61, 96, 134, 138, 157
Endler, 165
English, 23, 151, 163
environment, 28, 138
erudite scholar, 10
etiology, 22, 23, 27, 164
examples, 28, 63, 98, 132, 148
exhibit, 24, 79
Exorcism: Demon possession, 68
exorcist, 24
EXTERNAL DISSOCIATION IDENTITY CHECK LIST OBSERVED BY OTHERS, 158
External Dissociative, 29
external stimulations, 30
fainting, 28
faith perspective, 10
fallen, 23
family, 18, 27, 29, 30, 57, 77, 96, 113, 122, 128
favorable prognosis, 30

fear, 27, 33, 58, 85, 97, 155
features, 23, 164
fierce advocate, 10
final, 18, 38, 41, 51, 70, 74, 83, 87, 98, 111, 119, 121, 143, 146, 150, 151, 153
Fine, C. G, 162
first person singular "I, 24
Flora, *E. W.*, 162
fluctuating, 24
focus, 29, 53, 142
followers, 23
foreign spirit, 24
Franz Anton Mesmer, 23
frequency, 24
Freudian psychoanalysis, 33
friend,.28
FULLY INTEGRATED FEMALE, 129
fusion, 9, 17, 19, 26, 32, 33, 38, 41, 42, 43, 46, 51, 53, 54, 55, 57, 58, 60, 61, 73, 74, 75, 76, 77, 78, 82, 83, 87, 91, 94, 97, 98, 99, 101, 106, 107, 111, 119, 120, 124, 143, 146, 150, 151, 153
Fusion, 18, 32, 33, 46, 53, 62
Geriatric male suddenly regresses to early childlike behaviors, 79
Geriatric Treatment Center at Eastern State Hospital in Williamsburg, Virginia, 16
Giesbrecht T, 25
Giesbrecht, T, 163
Gillig, P. M, 162
Gleaves, D. H, 162
God, 43, 45, 52, 57, 60, 61, 62, 65, 69, 70, 71, 75, 76, 85, 102, 104, 113, 128, 129, 133
God's blessing, 45
grace of God, 16, 136
grandmother, 27
greater life experience, 18
Greek, 23, 97
Greeks, 23
Ground Rules, 39
groups, 19
Hallucinations, 143
happy, 18, 54, 109, 136, 138
hardworking, 18
head, 22
headache, 32, 110, 113, 117, 125, 136
health, 3, 9, 18, 22, 25, 26, 28, 50, 81, 95, 134, 155
Helier, S, 164
helter-skelter, 28
higher end of the intellectual scale., 28
Hippocrates, 23
Hippocratic Oath, 9
HISTORICAL BACKGROUND, 22
Holy Spirit, 69
Homicidal alters, 72
human development, 28
Humpty Dumpty, 55, 61
husband, 19, 49, 58, 59, 60, 68, 127, 131, 132, 134, 136
HUSBAND'S EXPERIENCE, 127
hypnosis, 22, 23, 29, 34, 37, 45, 56, 97, 114, 122, 147, 161
hypnotikos, 23
hypnotism, 23, 24

hysteria, 22, 23
Hysteria, 23
Hysterical, 23
Hysterical psychosis, 23
ICT/CT, 31
ideomotor response, 31
ideomotor responses, 31
imagery employed in therapy, 10
in thing, 23
incorporates, 23
increased, 17, 23
individual, 19, 24, 36, 44, 77, 87, 138, 144, 146, 155
INDIVIDUAL DISSOCIATION IDENTITY CHECK LIST, 157
induced somnambulism, 23
induction, 33, 37, 114, 117, 122
initiated, 28, 33, 116
innate, 27, 84, 148
insignificant events, 28
integration, 10, 18, 19, 26, 39, 41, 49, 70, 77, 93, 103, 106, 110, 131, 142, 146, 152, 153
Integration, 32
intelligent, 22, 71, 106, 148
intensity, 24
interest, 22, 81, 98, 145
intergenerational, 27, 148
interjects, 19, 34, 65, 66, 67, 69, 72, 74, 98, 99, 103, 105, 106, 118
Interjects, 34, 65
Internal Co-therapist, 31
internally configuring, 29
interprets, 28

INTERVIEW, DIAGNOSIS AND TREATMENT, 141
INTRODUCTION, 18
in-vivo desensitization" I was taught in graduate school. It was too exhausting for both client, 18
involuntary, 27, 58
irretrievably, 23
isolation, 23
James Braid, 23
James City County, Va, 26
Jean-Martin Charcot's, 23
Jesus, 24, 52, 65, 69, 70, 71
job,, 28
join the alter to the core, 93
kept off balance, 102
Kihlstrom, J. F., 162
kill off, 41
Kluft, 39, 41, 42, 162, 163
knowledgeable, 60, 155
Kohlenberg, R. J, 163
Kritchevsky, M, 163
Kurt Schneider, 25, 30
Language, 23, 163
Lanius, R, 161
lesson, 22, 89, 108
Libido, 114
life events, 28
life history, 28
life-threatening, 27
light trance, 56
Lilienfeld SO, 25
Lilienfeld, S. O, 163
limited life-experienced alters", 18
Living in poverty, 112
Lloyd, 165
locked, 22, 88

Loewenstein, R. J., 161
loss of a child, 28
lynchpin, 33
Lynn, S, 163
Lynn, S. J, 163
Lynn, SJ, 25
MacDonald, K, 163
major, 28, 146
Maldonado, J. R, 163
Maldonado, JR, 25
man, 23, 69, 71, 80, 101, 102, 109, 110, 128
Mark, 23, 24, 69
Marmar, 165
marriage, 28, 118
married, 49, 51, 62, 113, 127, 134
marsupial, 27
master's degree, 17
May, M. C, 162
McNary, S. W, 161
mechanical, 18
mechanism, 29, 34, 63, 94, 106
medical, 23, 25, 79, 95
medication, 26, 79, 96, 115
mediums, 24
mental health facility, 22
mental health professionals, 18
Merckelbach H, 25
Merckelbach, H.,, 163
Mesmer's, 23
mesmerism, 22, 23
middle-aged, 42, 49, 51, 95, 103, 106, 110, 112, 114
mind, 22, 27, 28, 29, 31, 32, 34, 35, 36, 37, 38, 42, 43, 45, 56, 57, 59, 60, 61, 65, 66, 67, 68, 74, 78, 79, 83, 84, 88, 89, 90, 91, 92, 93, 94, 97, 102, 105, 106, 108, 111, 113, 116, 117, 118, 119, 123, 126, 131, 136, 137, 138, 139, 142, 145, 146, 149, 150, 151, 152, 153, 154, 157, 165
minor event, 28
misdiagnosis, 25
mixed blessing, 53
Morton Prince's, 25
mother, 27, 49, 51, 53, 59, 66, 67, 83, 85, 99, 103, 104, 105, 107, 108, 112, 119, 123, 134, 139, 158
MOTHER APPROACHING THE END OF THE INTEGRATION PROCESS, 135
Mother Earth, 46, 47
Mother-in-law with her hands tightly wrapped around my clients neck, 106
multiple, 16, 32, 40, 50, 56, 65, 83, 145, 162, 164, 165
my, 5, 7, 16, 17, 22, 26, 27, 30, 31, 32, 34, 35, 36, 37, 38, 42, 43, 47, 49, 50, 51, 52, 53, 54, 55, 56, 57, 58, 59, 60, 61, 62, 63, 65, 67, 68, 69, 70, 71, 73, 74, 75, 76, 77, 80, 81, 82, 86, 88, 89, 91, 92, 93, 94, 95, 96, 97, 98, 99, 102, 103, 104, 107, 108, 109, 110, 111, 112, 113, 114, 116, 117, 118, 119, 121, 124, 125, 126, 127, 128, 129, 130, 131, 132, 133, 134, 135, 136, 137,

138, 139, 141, 143, 144, 146, 147, 148, 149, 151, 153, 154, 155
Myrick, A. C, 161
Nancy Mary Jane Flora, 5
natural disaster, 28
negative affect, 18, 36, 41, 42, 75, 77, 92, 151, 154
net, 22
Neurosis, 23
new-conscious mind, 28
newly, 18, 53, 131
nine-shot 22- caliber revolver, 16
non-conscious, 28
none, 18, 150
Norton, 25, 164
now new-conscious mind, 28
NURSE AND MOTHER, 131
observe, 28, 75, 93, 117
occultism, 23
occurrences, 27, 128
on Barnes & Noble's, 16
ONE, 63
one level of consciousness, 29
Oneness vs. Divided Mind, 34
open mind, 22
opossum, 27
orgasmic, 125
original conclusions, 17
Original Personality, 33
original theories, 17
overactive ability, 27
Oxford University Press, Oxford Index, 25, 164
Pain, C, 161
painlessly, 18

Panicking while seated on the floor of a truck, 121
paralyzed, 28
paramount, 24
parent, 28, 59, 88, 99, 146, 148, 158
parents, 28, 32, 65, 82, 99, 112, 147
PERSONAL BACKGROUND, 16
personal history, 28, 97
personal identity, 28
personal testimonies, 19
phenomenon, 18, 20, **22**, 23, 25, 27, 99, 144, 147, 155
physical appearance, 24
physician, 23, 114
Pinocchio, 55, 61
playmates, 28
Poplar Creek Psychological and Counseling Centre in Norge, Virginia,, 16
popularity, 23
possess, 24, 25, 27, 36, 109, 151
possessed, 23, 24, 35, 70, 71, 105, 144
possession, 22, 24, 25, 67, 68, 70
possum, 27
POSTLUDE, 155
Post-Traumatic Stress, 58
power struggles, 95
practice., 23
pragmatist, 10
PREFACE, 9
Presenting Personality, 33
Prevalence, 26
primary, 27, 28, 36, 63, 80,

81, 106, 142
Prince, M, 163
principal defense mechanism, 28
prior, 28, 29, 33, 53, 79, 115, 127, 158
prizes, 23
professional, 10
progresses, 18, 35, 46, 90, 116, 142, 150
projected, 32
Protector/Guardian, 32
pseudo alters, 34
pseudo time distortion, 33
psychiatrist, 25, 79, 80, 95, 96, 117, 118, 119
psychotic, 23, 30, 144
Putnam, 30, 41, 161
quality., 23
quantity, 23
Random House Dictionary, 23, 163
REFERENCES, 161
relive the trauma, 18
removed, 18, 37, 42, 50, 66, 67, 69, 73, 74, 75, 77
RESISTANCE TO CHANGE:, 63
resistive alter, 47
resolving the problem, 29
re-traumatizing, 17, 18, 75, 155
Reverse Installation, 34, 67, 74
revivification, 41, 43
Rhue, J. W., 163
Richard Kluft, 29, 39, 42
Richard Kluft M.D., 29, 42
Rose, 25

Ross, 39, 40, 41, 164
Rounsaville, 165
sage advice, 29
Satan, as a four-legged impish rat-goat, 103
satanic cult, 16, 34, 65, 67, 68, 69
satanic cult alter, 16
schizophrenia, 25, 26
schizophrenic voices, 30
Schizophrenic voices, 30
Schuengel,, 165
scientific, 23
screaming, 23, 71, 80, 136
secondary gain, 24, 97
secular perspective., 10
Secular Version.", 47
self-mutilation, 23, 88
senior psychologist, 16
separated, 28, 55, 94, 108, 133, 149, 150
shamans, 24
Shapiro, 41, 164
shock, 28, 72, 103, 128, 137
shoplifting, 17
Shoplifting joke backfires, 80
Simeon D, 161
SITUATIONS TO AVOID, 93
skepticism, 22
skeptics, 22
sleep-inducing narcotic, 23
Snyder, C. R, 164
social, 9, 23
Somnambulistic, 24
son, 27, 65, 99
SOUL/SOULS, 35
Southern Baptist, 69
Southwestern Virginia

Mental Health Institute in Marion, Virginia., 16
speaking in tongues, 24
SPECIAL TECHNIQUES, 65
Spiegel D, 25
Spiegel, D, 163
spoke, 24, 58, 105, 154
spontaneous fusion, 18, 77
Spontaneous possession, 24
spontaneously, 24, 36, 51, 76, 77, 95, 145, 157, 158
Squire, L. R, 163
Steel, 41, 164
Steinberg, 165
stodgy, 10
STRANGE SITUATIONS, 101
strength, 24, 58, 62, 90, 127, 158
stress, 28, 128, 132, 161, 165
subconscious mind, 18, 27, 28, 29, 31, 32, 36, 65, 71, 79, 84, 93, 94, 102, 108, 115, 116, 126, 150, 153
Subconscious Mind, 31
survive, 28, 57, 63, 109, 146, 150
switching, 29, 86, 127, 129, 130, 150
SWITCHING, 29
Synergism, 32
Taylor and Martin, 25
technique, 9, 10, 17, 18, 19, 34, 39, 40, 41, 42, 50, 51, 65, 67, 83, 109, 134, 136, 137, 138, 139, 141, 152, 154, 161
techniques, 17, 19, 29, 31, 54, 61, 67, 70, 88, 95, 148, 155, 162
temper tantrum.', 59
test of time, 18
TESTIMONIALS, 127
The Beginnings, 22
THE CHALLENGE, 39
THE FIRST AND LONGEST SUCCESSFUL INTEGRATION, 130
The four systems are, 30
The Problem, 22
THE PROCESS, 41
The Rise of Disintegrated Personality, 25
Then They Were One, 9
theological, 35, 65, 71
therapeutic techniques, 17
therapist, 9, 17, 18, 31, 34, 35, 51, 56, 60, 63, 67, 88, 91, 97, 99, 100, 106, 108, 116, 117, 121, 142, 143, 145, 147, 151, 152
Therapist-induced interject, 67
therapy, 9, 18, 26, 30, 33, 34, 35, 39, 47, 50, 53, 55, 56, 61, 63, 73, 80, 82, 84, 86, 90, 95, 96, 103, 106, 109, 111, 112, 121, 128, 131, 139, 141, 142, 143, 145, 146, 147, 148, 150, 151, 152, 153, 161, 162, 164
Thigpen, 25, 97, 165
Thigpen and Cleckley, 25, 97
three successive stages of hypnosis: "lethargy, catalepsy and somnambulism, 24

time heal all wounds, 43
too stressful, 28
too young, 47
toy, 28, 158
Tracing the Historical Development of the Diagnosis and Treatment of Multiple Personality Disorder in 19th and 20th Century North America.", 17
Traité du Somnambulism, 23
traits, 23, 29
TRANSITIONAL CASE EXAMPLES, 42, 49
traumatizing, 27, 99, 118
Trial Fusion, 33
tried-and-true, 18
True Identity, 38
Tsai, M, 163
Two clinched fists, 122
Type, 23
U.S. Population, 26
Unabridged, 23, 163
unclean spirit, 69
unconsciously, 27
uncontrolled, 23
understanding, 27, 29, 31, 35, 43, 45, 69, 76, 84, 117, 128, 133, 134, 150
unnecessary suffering, 50
unreality, 44
unreflective peers, 10
uterus, 23
Vaihinger,, 44, 165
VALIDATION, 97
Van der Kolk, 165
Van Ijzendoorn, 165
Vernon Grounds, B.A., B.D. and Ph.D, 7
Virgin Mary and three others, 108
voluntary, 24
wandering, 23
Weiten, 165
Whether to join a sleeping alter, 82
White light felt like mint toothpaste, 101
wild speculation, 23
win-win, 17
wisdom, 28, 77, 109, 148
witch doctors, 24
workshops, 17
world, 22, 31, 34, 53, 67, 120, 130, 135, 148, 149
World Population, 26
Wozney, 25, 164
Yapko, 43, 165
young minds., 28
Zeidner,, 165